CW00958574

THE LONDON OF
JACK THE RIPPER
THEN AND NOW

THE LONDON OF
JACK THE RIPPER

THEN AND NOW

ROBERT CLACK AND PHILIP HUTCHINSON

FOREWORD BY STEWART P. EVANS

breedon **books**
PUBLISHING

First published in Great Britain in 2007 by
The Breedon Books Publishing Company Limited
Breedon House, 3 The Parker Centre,
Derby, DE21 4SZ.

DEDICATION FROM THE AUTHORS

Robert Clack:
For my mother and to the memory of my father, Andrew Clack.

Philip Hutchinson:
For Richard Jones, who believes in my guiding abilities, and to Diddles,
for being a cat of unquestionable mischief.

ISBN 978-1-85983-600-2

Printed and bound by Cromwell Press, Trowbridge, Wiltshire.

CONTENTS

Ripper's Corner, Mitre Square, from *The Pictorial World*,
11 October 1888.

FOREWORD

Despite the frequent appearance of new books touching on the subject of Jack the Ripper, it is not very often that one that may be considered 'necessary' is published. This, happily, is one of those volumes. There can be few people able to equal the combined knowledge of these two authors on their chosen subject. To accompany them on a tour of the area haunted by Jack the Ripper in 1888 is to know that you are in safe hands and that you are benefiting from their great knowledge. Both are dedicated researchers and guides.

The East End of London and that part of the great City that touches upon it, Aldgate, are forever tainted by the shadow of the unknown Victorian murderer whose name still strikes the individual with both fear and fascination. The name Whitechapel is virtually synonymous with that of Jack the Ripper – indeed, his first press exposure hailed him as 'The Whitechapel Murderer'. The large number of tourists who are still guided around the area every week testifies to this continuing fascination. Yet what do they seek? There is little of Jack's original Victorian London to be seen today, although some buildings, such as the Princess Alice and Ten Bells pubs, the Buck's Row Board School, the frontage of the Crispin Street night refuge and the imposing London Hospital are still to be seen. The railway arches at Pinchin Street and Swallow Gardens still evoke the grim atmosphere of the time, as do a few other obscure corners of this historic area.

But slum clearance, begun in the late 1800s, the devastation wrought by the Luftwaffe during World War Two and modern urban development have all taken their toll. Visiting the area in the 1960s I was lucky enough to find a little-changed Mitre Square bordered by grim warehouses; the dark and brooding George Yard Buildings; narrow Durward Street (formerly Buck's Row) lined with Victorian terraced dwellings, whose mute walls had seen Jack the Ripper at work. Perhaps the most impressive sight, for a student of the Ripper crimes, was the grimy brick, terraced dwelling that was 29 Hanbury Street, still looking much as it did in 1888; apart from the 'N. Brill' hairdresser's sign and advertisements for Vaseline and Brylcreem at the front. I was able to try the front door, with its tattered coat of peeling pale green paint – knowing that the terrifying Jack had passed through that very portal.

All these places have now disappeared, having been demolished and built upon in the large-scale urban improvement of the late 1960s and early 1970s. However, it is still possible to visit the locations where they stood and to evoke a mental image of what it must have been like in those long-gone days. In this book your trusty guides will take you on a trip around the killing grounds of Jack the Ripper's London. They will guide you to the exact spots using photographs and illustrations and you will be able to locate and mentally recreate the scenes of long ago. It should be noted that it is solely due to the dedicated research of these two authors that many of these images are seen here for the first time. It is not often that I see such new material – but they have amazed and delighted me. It is a book that I shall treasure in my collection.

Stewart P. Evans

Cambridgeshire, July 2007.

INTRODUCTION

Picture this scenario: a distant bell tolls the stroke of midnight. A lone pretty, well-dressed young woman walks down a busy London street, struggling to see the numerous streetlights through the thick fog. She turns into a dark alleyway, lit by a single flickering gas lamp, and suddenly a shadowy figure blocks her path. He is tall, wearing a cape and a top hat. In one hand he holds a large Gladstone bag. From beneath his cloak he slowly retrieves a dagger. The young woman screams as he plunges the knife into her chest again and again. She crumples to the ground and the silent assassin runs into the cover of the night.

This is what most people would imagine whenever the name of the quintessential bogeyman, Jack the Ripper, is mentioned. The fact of the matter is that almost every detail of this image bears no relation to reality and is all part of the populist myth created through decades of pulp fiction and movies. One thing from the above description rings true, however: the dark alleyway and that dim gas lamp. At the time of the Ripper murders much of the East End of London was a rat-run of unlit alleys and passages, squalid by day and treacherous by night. Almost all of these locations have changed beyond recognition, with the area undergoing regeneration even today. Not only have most of the buildings been obliterated, but in many cases even the very streets on which they stood now also lie under offices and housing estates.

In this volume, we will attempt to bring the past and present a little closer together and present you with a topographical overview of the relevant locations never previously undertaken. A basic summary of the case is provided if you are a new student of Ripperology. For those more experienced criminological devotees, we are providing not only a wealth of images of places that bore witness to the presence of the major players in this drama, as they look today, but also an extensive series of photographs and illustrations that have rarely been seen before. Such items were frequently acquired through the meticulous searching of archive services and are often from the authors' personal collections.

Among the most impressive illustrations is a series of photographs taken by the amateur criminologist John Gordon Whitby in September 1961. They were acquired for this book through the generosity of his niece Margaret Whitby-Green, a friend of one of the authors. Like long-forgotten documents, this group of photographs lay in a drawer in Lincolnshire for decades and here you will be able to see many of them for the very first time. Of particular note to the serious researcher is the fact that Whitby accurately identified the anonymous railway arch under which Frances Coles

John Gordon Whitby, who took a series of photographs of the locations in September, 1961.
(Courtesy Margaret Whitby-Green)

died in February 1891 nearly half a century before the rest of the Ripper world rediscovered its correct location after a period of intensive research.

The authors would like to thank the following for their kind assistance in the preparation of this book: Stewart P. Evans, Caroline Morris, Margaret Whitby-Green, Colin Roberts, Christopher Lloyd and Malcolm Barr-Hamilton (Tower Hamlets Library), Richard Whittington-Egan, Brian Girling, Dr Kenneth Thomas (Truman's archive), Richard Jones, Michael Dummer, David Cawley, Debra J. Arif, John Bennett, Bernard Brown and Jake Luukanen.

We would also like to extend our gratitude to Stephen P. Ryder and the posters on Casebook (www.casebook.org), the world's leading Internet Ripper resource, and to our colleagues at The Whitechapel Society 1888 (www.whitechapelsociety.com) for their friendship, support and inspiration.

Before 'The Macnaghten Five'

The Jack the Ripper murders occurred in London in 1888. This was the year after Queen Victoria's Golden Jubilee and the publication of the first Sherlock Holmes novel. On 3 October 1888, Gilbert and Sullivan produced their first performance of the operetta *Yeomen of the Guard*. It was also the year of the invention of Kodak film and the revolving door, the year that the first live concert sound recording was made, and the year of the first publication of *National Geographic* magazine.

The following year, the social reformer Charles Booth published his *Descriptive Map of London Poverty*, a huge undertaking that was never fully completed in any detail outside sections of the East End. The various maps resembled many other London street maps, with one major reservation: Booth and his researchers had meticulously shaded each house (and, when that became too impractical to achieve, each street) using different colours to denote the comparative wealth or poverty of each property's inhabitants. Many of the backstreets of the East End (though not most of the major thoroughfares and arteries, where the residents tended to be lower-middle class shopkeepers) were coloured blue or black, signifying 'vicious; semi-criminal'. Pollution was high and smoke from the West End frequently blew over to the east and covered the buildings in grime, shortening an already limited life expectancy for many.

Poverty in parts of the East End was extreme in a way it is impossible to contemplate in London today. The building expansion within the City of London, largely consisting of business premises, had pushed the central populace further east into an already overcrowded part of the capital. The situation was exacerbated by the displacement of the Eastern European Jews, fleeing the pogroms in Russia and genocide in Upper Silesia. Many fled to the East End of London as it encompassed the docks, where their ships would arrive, and was home to two ancient synagogues.

At that time, many East End streets were only wide enough to allow the passage of a hansom cab. Many of the houses were built over cesspits and the infant mortality rate was at a disastrous 55 percent. 900,000 people lived in the East End. Around a quarter of a million were based in Whitechapel, the area commonly associated with the Ripper murders, and at any one time 15,000 were classed as homeless. Prostitution was not a career choice; it was a financial necessity for women whose youthful charms had long ceased to be apparent and whose alcohol-ridden bodies were usually on sale for fourpence, the standard cost of a lodging-house bed for the night.

Those who had jobs were mostly casual dock labourers and porters, market traders, street sellers and sweatshop workers. However, the demand for employment always outstripped the available positions several times over. As a result, many hopeless and unoccupied individuals turned to drink to eliminate the reality of their dire existence. Life became a cycle of simply acquiring enough money that day to pay for a bed if your willpower was strong enough or just for another bottle of gin if you'd had a particularly depressing time. Money that could not be acquired from legitimate labour or through pawning possessions could be found via prostitution, theft or extortion. The violence and lawlessness of Charles Booth's worst slum districts was the result of social laissez-faire and a lack of philanthropy. An awareness of the conditions in which tens of thousands of people lived was only beginning to become apparent, though Henry Mayhew, General William Booth and even Charles Dickens had played their parts in bringing the squalid truth to an ignorant populace to whom the East End was an alien ghetto.

Jack the Ripper is sometimes referred to as being 'the world's first serial killer' but that is, of course, hugely erroneous. Serial killing existed for centuries beforehand and, in fact, two major Victorian poisoning cases – Mary Ann Cotton in Northumberland and William Palmer in Staffordshire – each had a body count far higher than that achieved by the Ripper.

It is important here to classify a clear division between the Jack the Ripper murders and the series of crimes collectively known as The Whitechapel Murders (even though several were not in Whitechapel itself). As nobody was ever brought to justice for the killings, we will never know the true number of women who died or were maimed at his (and it is fairly safe to say it was a 'he', in spite of some of the more bizarre theories) hands. Estimates range from three to nearly 20 victims. Most books and television documentaries abide by the opinion of Sir Melville Macnaghten who, in 1894, forwarded a memorandum naming five women as those most likely to have been the victims of Jack the Ripper. The so-called 'canonical five' were accepted as fact for decades and it is only in recent years that some have started to challenge that assertion. Some claim more possible victims (such as Martha Tabram and Alice McKenzie) while others question the legitimacy of two of the five (suggesting Elizabeth Stride was killed in a domestic incident and Mary Jane Kelly died at the hand of a copycat killer). Jack the Ripper is not responsible for all The Whitechapel Murders and few people have thought so for many, many years. However, for the sake of completeness in this volume we will be covering all the crimes attributed to him at one time or another in the East End. This means the exclusion of three other victims who died elsewhere: Elizabeth Jackson, whose dismembered body was found in the Thames; 'The Whitehall Mystery', in which a torso was discovered recently dumped in the partially constructed cellars of

New Scotland Yard near the Thames Embankment; and the murder of Carrie Brown in New York in April 1891. All these cases have been linked to Jack the Ripper at some point, but they are outside the locale in which he undoubtedly lived and killed.

ANNIE MILLWOOD

It is of interest to note that the precedent for The Whitechapel Murders took place just a matter of yards from the location where the most infamous of the killings, that of Mary Jane Kelly, occurred. White's Row is a fairly narrow street, early 18th century in origin, bordered on the west by the junctions of Bell Lane, Crispin Street and Artillery Lane and on the east by the major artery of Commercial Street. Although the north side has now been completely rebuilt as part of White's Row multi-storey car park, a few of the original buildings – some approaching 200 years of age – still remain on the south. Halfway along the southern end of White's Row stands a modern block of apartments, built over the location of the temporary address of the woman many believe to have been the first possible victim of Jack the Ripper.

White's Row looking east, c.1940. In the distance, the Queen's Head pub can be seen.
(Courtesy Tower Hamlets Local History Library and Archives)

White's Row, 2007.

Annie Millwood was a widow, previously married to a soldier named Richard. There is no reference to any woman of the correct age in the London area named Annie Millwood in the Census for 1881, nor indeed of a married couple matching their names anywhere in England. However, there is a single Fanny Millwood married to a Richard Millwood (born in Hampshire in 1842) listed as resident in St Pancras and working as a decorator. He cannot be found in the 1861 Census, which does tend to make the suggestion that he had previously been a solider more likely. The return gives her an approximate birth date of 1841 in the same district. In the previous 1871 Census she is again listed as Fanny and both names no longer show on the 1891 Census, so it is likely that history has incorrectly recorded her name and we are looking at an attack upon a woman named Frances Millwood. Not only this, but from the Census returns we can establish more information on 'Annie'. Fanny was actually 47 at the time of the attack, not 38 as she told the Infirmary. While living at 8 Bath Row in St Pancras in 1880 they had a son in whom they called George. After the death of Richard, George was moved to Hampshire and brought up by his father's family. As a young man, George returned to live in London before 1901.

Now widowed and entrenched in middle-age, without an income, it is possible that Millwood had gravitated towards the cheaper East End of London. Having slipped further down the social ladder, she may have been forced to survive by prostitution but this cannot be known for certain. 8 White's Row was one of almost countless low-grade lodging houses situated in the area. It went by the rather grand name of Spitalfields Chambers, but 'Chambers' was, in fact, a suffix given to many of the doss houses.

Spitalfields Chambers, 8 White's Row, from *The Illustrated Police News*, 28 February 1891.

At 5pm on Saturday 25 February 1888, Annie Millwood was admitted to the Whitechapel Union Infirmary, close to the eastern extremity of Hanbury Street and on Baker's Row (now called Vallance Road – the location of the home of the notorious Kray Twins). It was designed by the architect Thomas D. Barry and built in 1858. The name was changed to St Peter's Hospital in 1924. After suffering considerable damage from the Luftwaffe in World War Two, it was demolished in the 1950s. Although the cause of admission is recorded as simply 'stabs', Millwood had in fact been subjected to an intense attack

The site of 8 White's Row, 2007.

upon the lower half of her body. She told staff that the man who attacked her was a stranger and had simply drawn out a clasp knife, with which he repeatedly stabbed her in the trunk and legs in an unprovoked incident. It appears that there were no witnesses to the assault.

From this distance, we will never know where or even when the actual attack took place. However,

Whitechapel Union Infirmary, situated on the eastern side of Baker's Row (to the right in this view), 19 April 1913.

it is unlikely that such a vicious maiming would have been anything other than very recent. It is hard to imagine why a woman suffering from deep multiple stab wounds would not have sought medical attention as soon as possible. If we are to assume that Millwood had only just been stabbed and that there were supposedly no witnesses to the assault, then it is perfectly likely that the

Shepherd's Place archway from White's Row, c.1909. Built around 1810, the arch was located on the southern side of White's Row at its western end.

attack took place in one of the residential backstreets very close to 8 White's Row. These included Tenter Street (only a single bonding warehouse from this time survives), Shepherd Street (now Toynbee Street), Butler Street (now Brune Street) and Emert's Place.

Millwood recovered from this attack and was discharged to South Grove Workhouse on the Mile End Road four weeks later, on 21 March. While working at the rear of the building on 31 March she suddenly fell to the floor and died. Coroner Wynne Baxter concluded in April that she had died as a result of ulceration. Her attack, it seems, played no part in her death.

ADA WILSON

A month after the attack upon Annie Millwood, another frenzied stabbing incident took place one and a half miles further east, just off the current A11 (Mile End Road). This is some distance from where the other crimes occurred.

Ada Wilson was the only person included in the list of victims who was known to have had regular employment as a machinist. She was 39 years old and lived at 19 Maidmans Street, off

An illustration from *The Illustrated Police News*, 7 April 1888, showing the attack on Ada Wilson.

ESCAPE OF THE ASSASSIN

ATTEMPTED MURDER AT BOW

Maidman Street, *c.1950*. A general view of a street now completely obliterated. This type of housing was typical and many such houses still survive in East London.

Burdett Road in Mile End. At half past midnight on 28 March 1888 she was preparing herself for bed when a man knocked on her door. She was able to give a fairly detailed description of her assailant. He appeared to be aged around 30, 5ft 6in in height, with a fair moustache and a sunburnt face. He was wearing a 'wideawake' hat (similar in style to the ancient Quaker hats), light trousers and a dark coat. The intruder demanded money from Wilson and told her if she refused he would kill her immediately.

Ada Wilson called his bluff, but the attacker remained true to his word and pulled out a clasp knife with which he proceeded to stab Wilson twice in the throat. Her screams brought assistance from another resident of 19 Maidmans Street named Rose Bierman. Upon running down the stairs she found Ada Wilson in a state of partial undress. Wilson cried out to her 'Stop that man for cutting my throat; he has stabbed me'. The knifeman ran from the scene of the crime and was never subsequently traced. It is likely that had Bierman not arrived so quickly, Ada Wilson would have been killed. A Dr Wheeler from Mile End Road treated Wilson's wounds, which were deemed life-threatening. She was taken to the London Hospital on Whitechapel Road where it was fully expected she would succumb to the wounds. However, she made a remarkable recovery and was discharged on 27 April.

It is almost certain that Wilson's attacker was not Jack the Ripper, although his description concurs in many ways with those given of the Ripper himself. Robbery was apparently the motive here (though it may have been a ruse as a precursor to a premeditated attack) and the incident took place much further east than the other crimes. Nevertheless, reportage on this case has found it forever linked peripherally to the later Ripper crimes.

EMMA SMITH

The particularly savage attack upon Emma Elizabeth Smith was the first of the actual Whitechapel Murders, as the attacks on Millwood and Wilson had not been fatal. Little is known of her past. She appears to have moved to London from an unspecified rural location and was either widowed

A lodging house in George Street, from *The Illustrated Police News*, 15 September 1888.

or separated from her husband. She told acquaintances that she had a son and daughter who lived in Finsbury Park, but this was never confirmed. Smith was 5ft 2in in height with a fair complexion, light brown hair, and a scar on her right temple. She was known to be a heavy drinker and prostitute. Unlike many transients, Smith had been a regular lodger at 18 George Street, Spitalfields, since the autumn of 1886. Shortly after the Ripper crimes, George Street was renamed Lolesworth Street (running north to south through the notorious colloquially-named 'Flower and Dean Estate'). The approximate position of part of George Street is now called Flower and Dean Walk, accessed from Wentworth Street.

At 12:15am on Tuesday 3 April 1888, Emma Smith was seen by Margaret Hames, a fellow George Street lodger (who had been punched in the face by two strangers only a few minutes previously), at the junction of Farrance Street and Burdett Road, very close to where Commercial Road becomes the East India Dock Road near the Thames. Smith was talking to a man in a dark coat and white scarf, who most certainly had no connection to the subsequent events. By Smith's own account, at 1:30am she was passing the church of St Mary Matfelon, Whitechapel, probably having walked the entire length of the Commercial Road to get there. The original Mediaeval church (from which Whitechapel got its name) was built in around 1270, enlarged in the 1500s and mostly rebuilt around the time of the Reformation. This was demolished in 1875 and the replacement church was consecrated on 2 February 1877. Just three years later it was destroyed in a fire, although the tower and spire were largely undamaged. The rebuilt nave and chancel were consecrated on 1 December 1882. The church was a highly impressive and imposing building, the enormous spire visible along the Whitechapel Road and Whitechapel High Street. It was gutted by incendiary bombs on 29 December 1940, the clock hands freezing at 2.45, and the ruins were not demolished until well over a decade later. Today a few tombstones remain, and the outline of the original church has been marked out in concrete slabs. The open grassland has been renamed Altab Ali Park, a memorial to a Bengali clothing merchant who was murdered nearby in 1978.

It was here that Emma Smith saw three men approaching her, one still a teenager. Their demeanour made her feel uneasy, and she crossed the street and made her way north up Osborn Street to avoid them. However, they followed her and as she crossed to the west side of the street she began to run. At this point, the gang ran after her. She was caught by the men at the junctions of Wentworth Street, Old Montague Street, Osborn Street and Brick Lane (probably on the south side of the street where Osborn Street meets Wentworth Street), robbed and subjected to a horrifying assault. She was literally about one minute's walk from the door of 18 George Street.

St Mary's Church, Whitechapel
Road, c.1900.

Whitechapel High Street in 1899, in a view looking east from the junction with Commercial Street.
(Courtesy Tower Hamlets Local History Library and Archives)

The press reports claim that after finally reaching George Street she did not leave the lodging house until 4 or 5am, in the company of Mary Russell, the deputy, to be taken to the London Hospital. It was evident the assault had been barbaric. Her face was very badly bruised and her right ear was partially torn off. As Smith and Russell (along with another resident named Annie Lee) passed Taylor's cocoa factory on the junction of Brick Lane and Wentworth Street, Smith had commented that it was opposite where she had been attacked. Smith had voiced objections to being taken to hospital and would not discuss what had happened to her.

Osborn Street looking towards Brick Lane, *c.*1902.

Brick Lane from Osborn Street, 2007. Smith was probably attacked at the bottom left of the picture.

Brick Lane, 1895.

Old Montague Street from Wentworth Street, September 1961. *(Courtesy Margaret Whitby-Green)*

Old Montague Street from Wentworth Street, 2007.

Whitechapel Road in 1895, showing the London Hospital on the right.

Upon arrival, she was admitted and attended to by Dr George Haslip, the House Surgeon. An unknown blunt object, most likely a stick, had been thrust with such force into her vagina that it had ripped through some of her internal organs. Smith died of peritonitis only a few hours later, at 9am.

Because Emma Smith was murdered by a gang who robbed and beat her, it is extremely unlikely that this killing has any connection with the Ripper crimes. However, when the autumn of 1888 came around, the newspapers began to refer to this attack and viewed it as the beginning of the series, for no other reason than the victim had been a prostitute who was murdered by an unknown party in the middle of Whitechapel. Several street gangs roamed the area, extorting money with violence – particularly from prostitutes. However, the attack on Smith was extreme. The blame has been placed at the door of the group colloquially referred to today as The Old Nichol Gang, who were supposedly a particularly distasteful group of thugs from a short way north, near Shoreditch. No documented evidence has been found that this gang ever existed, but some groups of street thugs were referred to as 'High Rip' gangs.

The police were not informed of the murder until several days later, on 6 April, and even then

The Receiving Room at The London Hospital, *c.*1900 *(Courtesy Michael Dummer)*

only because the Coroner's Office was informing them of the inquest due to be held the following day. Inspector Edmund Reid, the Local Inspector for Whitechapel, headed the investigation for the Metropolitan Police. Not a single constable had witnessed the attack or even the agonised final walk Smith had taken in the company of Russell and Lee towards the London Hospital, half a mile further east.

MARTHA TABRAM

Martha Tabram was born Martha White in 1849. By the time she was 16 her parents had seperated and her father, unable to work through infirmity, was living in St George's Road. Just when they were beginning a period of reconciliation, her father dropped dead in November 1865. Martha, the youngest child, was married by the age of 19 and had already developed a taste for alcohol that was to plague and taint the rest of her life. She married Henry Samuel Tabram

Mortuary photograph of Martha Tabram. *(Courtesy Stewart P. Evans)*

on 25 December 1869 and the couple had two sons – Frederick John in 1871 and Charles Henry late the following year. By this time they were living at 20 Marshall Street, close to Martha's childhood home.

By 1875 the couple had split, largely due to Martha's excessive drinking. For the following few years, Henry supported Martha with 12 shillings a week, but reduced this to only two shillings and sixpence when her harassment of him became excessive and she began to cohabit with another man named Henry Turner. Although she stayed with him for the rest of her life, she was not a good companion. A great deal of money she acquired was spent on drink and on occasions she was given to having hysterical fits or seizures when particularly inebriated.

By 1888, Martha was 37 years old, 5ft 3in tall and overweight. Both she and Turner were earning a living as street traders and lodged with William and Mary Bousfield at 4 Star Place, off Star Street in Commercial Road (long since demolished, but now at the end of Hainton Close). Mrs Bousfield was later to relate that Martha generally sold matches, although she also suspected she had been earning by prostitution. In late June the pair absconded without notice or paying

The location of Star Place, 2007.

Aldgate Pump looking towards Leadenhall Street, 1895.

due rent. Martha secretly returned later to leave the key. After a couple of weeks, Martha and Henry had split. She now stayed in a common lodging house at 19 George Street. The last time Turner saw Tabram was in Leadenhall Street, only a couple of days before she died. She was now destitute and he gave her a small sum of money to support herself.

Monday 6 August 1888 was a Bank Holiday and consequently many people found themselves in the pubs celebrating. Earlier in the evening, Martha had been in the company of a friend, a fellow prostitute commonly known as Pearly Poll, although her real name was Mary Ann Connelly. In the Two Brewers public house in Brick Lane they had met a pair of soldiers. For the rest of the evening they had been in and out of several pubs and were noticed by Tabram's sister-in-law (Ann Morris) entering the White Swan at 20 Whitechapel High Street at approximately 11pm. On leaving the pub, the two couples crossed the street and proceeded east into Whitechapel. They parted company at the entrance to George Yard (now Gunthorpe Street), next to the entrance to the White Hart pub. Mary Ann Connelly took her soldier a few yards further down

The Two Brewers, *c.1930s.* (*Courtesy Truman's Archive*)

the street to Angel Alley (which still exists in part) after watching Martha drunkenly stagger with her companion up George Yard in the direction of Wentworth Street.

George Yard Buildings was a large, red-bricked tenement block near the north-western end of George Yard (demolished in 1972, although a small fragment of wall remains attached to the rear

Whitechapel High Street looking west from Commercial Street, 1914.

Whitechapel High Street, 1899. The entrance to George Yard can be seen just to the left of centre. In the centre of the image is 'Ye Olde Angel' public house, to the right of which is the entrance to Angel Alley. *(Courtesy Tower Hamlets Local History Library and Archives)*

of the building on the corner of Wentworth Street). It is difficult today to understand the plan of the building and unfortunately there are no known internal images of it, but it appears that a large archway in the front wall preceded a short alley. At the end of the alley, an open doorway led to the staircase to the upper floors, which turned back on itself at the landings. Because of the easy access to the building and the relatively extensive open floor area outside individual dwellings, it was not at all unusual for the homeless to enter the building and sleep on the floors of the corridors to protect themselves from the elements.

Whitechapel High Street showing 'Ye Olde Angel', 1894.

Entrance to Angel Alley, 2007.

Alfred George Crow was a young cab driver and lived in Room 35 of George Yard Buildings and, on returning from work at approximately 3.30am on 7 August, he passed what he took in the darkness to be a sleeping woman on the first-floor landing. This being a familiar sight, he continued on his way and thought nothing unusual. Joseph and Elizabeth Mahoney lived at 47 George Yard Buildings and had seen no one there at 1.40am. By 4.45am the sun had begun to rise and John Saunders Reeves, a dock labourer living two doors from Crow at Room 37, was just leaving to start work himself. On coming to the first-floor staircase he found the body of a woman in a pool of blood. She had dark hair and was wearing a dress, green skirt, brown petticoat, long black jacket, brown stockings, side-spring boots and a black bonnet. All were in poor condition. There was no blood in her mouth, her hands were clenched and her clothing had been ripped up the front. The position of the body

Gunthorpe Street (formerly George Yard) looking north, 1967. *(Courtesy Stewart P. Evans)*

Gunthorpe Street looking north, 2004.

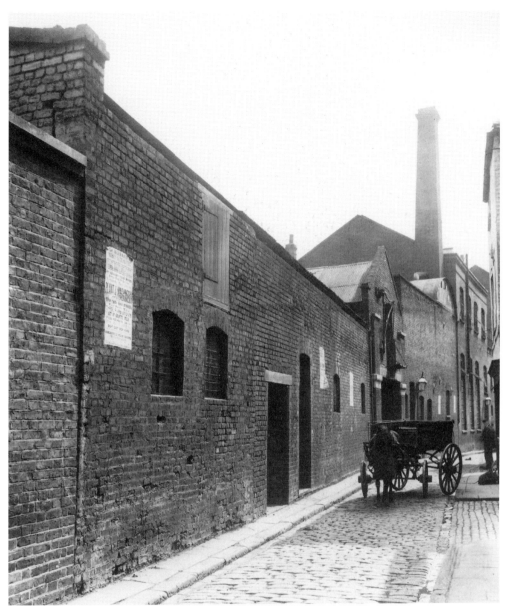

George Yard looking south, May 1898. *(Courtesy Richard Jones)*

suggested sexual intercourse had just taken place. Reeves ran to find a policeman and returned with PC Thomas Barrett 226H. At 2am, Barrett had been on patrol in George Yard where he met a Private of the Guards. The soldier had told the policeman he was waiting for a friend who had gone away with a girl. Upon seeing the corpse, Barrett sent for Dr Timothy Robert Killeen, resident at 68 Brick Lane, a few minutes walk north-east of George Yard.

Killeen arrived at approximately 5.30am and found a total of 39 stab wounds on the body. It appeared that 38 had been made with a penknife, but the 39th, to her breastbone, had been made with a bayonet or dagger. Modern forensics now discount the possibility of a bayonet having been used and even suggest that the way the skin yields to stab wounds means one single implement may have been responsible for all the injuries.

Tabram's body was removed to the Whitechapel Mortuary, which was for that brief period of time only a brick shed in Pavilion Yard, off Eagle Place in Old Montague Street, close to Baker's Row. The actual location of the shed itself is hard to

Entrance to George Yard Buildings, from *Jack the Ripper, A New Theory* by William Stewart, 1938.

George Yard Buildings, 1967. *(Courtesy Stewart P. Evans)*

Location of George Yard Buildings, 2004.

ascertain, but historians have managed to say with a degree of confidence that it overlay a now totally anonymous spot to the side of a footpath linking the modern houses in Regal Close and Moss Close. Killeen performed a post-mortem on the body and reached the conclusion that it was probably a right-handed individual who had inflicted the wounds. The dead woman was to remain officially unidentified for another week. At that time, photography was a very new addition to the tools at the disposal of the Metropolitan Police and images of deceased individuals were made purely for the purpose of identification should the remains begin to deteriorate without anyone stepping forward to give the dead person a name. There had been three women who had separately claimed to know the deceased, but each had given a different name.

On 9 August, Mary Ann Connelly went to Commercial Street Police Station and told the officers

An artists impression of the discovery of Martha Tabram's body, from *Famous Crimes Past and Present*, edited by Harold Furniss, 1903.

68 Brick Lane, 2007. The building marked 'GB Grambangla' was the home of Dr Killeen.

there that she had been drinking with her friend Emma Turner (one of Martha's aliases) on the night of 6 August. Local Inspector Reid was again unable to trace Tabram's movements for the period between when she was last seen by Connelly and the discovery of her body by Reeves. Connelly and PC Barrett were taken to both Wellington Barracks and the Tower of London in the hope of identifying the soldiers, given the description of their uniforms provided by Connelly. Those that Connelly did pick out had watertight alibis and it has since been suggested that

The Working Lads' Institute, Whitechapel Road, from *The Illustrated London News*, 7 November 1885.

The Working Lads' Institute, Whitechapel Road, 2007.

she was either mistaken or even falsified the clothing worn by the men. She was certainly seen as an unreliable witness.

The inquest was held at the Whitechapel Working Lads' Institute in Whitechapel Road (opposite the London Hospital and very close to the Tube station entrance) on 9 August. The building had only been opened in 1885 and was to host further inquests resulting from the Whitechapel Murders.

The interior of the Working Lads' Institute, from *Autumn of Terror* by Tom Cullen, 1965.

Although its purpose has changed – the ground floor now serving as a cut-price goods shop – it still remains largely the same on the outside.

It was not until 14 August that Tabram was finally identified by her estranged husband, Samuel. He had read in the newspapers the previous day that the woman found in George Yard Buildings was named Tabram. At present, no reports have been found of her funeral and her final resting-place is currently unknown.

MARY ANN NICHOLS

Mary Ann Nichols (commonly referred to as Polly Nichols), was born Mary Ann Walker on 26 August 1845 in Dawes Court, Shoe Lane, Fleet Street. She was the daughter of Edward and Caroline Walker. When she was 18, she married William Nichols and they had five children: Edward John (born 1866), Percy George (born 1868), Alice Esther (born 1870), Eliza Sarah (born 1877) and Henry Alfred (born 1879). The union ran into difficulties around 1877, when Mary Ann started drinking heavily and William Nichols had a brief affair with a nurse who assisted at the birth of Eliza Sarah. They separated on numerous occasions due to Mary Ann's alcohol consumption and William's infidelity. By about 1880 they had split permanently. The eldest son went to stay with Mary

Mortuary photograph of Mary Ann Nichols.
(Courtesy Stewart P. Evans)

Ann's father and the other four children stayed with William Nichols.

Mary Ann Nichols's movements after the break up of her marriage are extremely well documented. Her whereabouts are unknown from spring 1881 to spring 1882, but she spent much of the three years immediately following her separation in Lambeth Workhouse. Just before the last of these stays, she had attempted a reconciliation with her father, which failed after two months of cohabitation due to the friction caused by her drinking.

From 2 June 1883 she is said to have lived for four and a half years with a blacksmith named Thomas Drew, who had his own workshop in York Mews, 1 York Street, Walworth. During this time she had to attend the funeral of her brother, who had been burned to death in a paraffin explosion. It was noted that she appeared respectable at the service. However, by the end of October 1887 this relationship too had foundered and when Polly found herself back on the streets she was never to know a proper home again.

She is known to have spent brief periods at the workhouses in Lambeth, St Giles, The Strand and Mitcham over the next few months. For three weeks in December it is believed she was forced to sleep rough in Trafalgar Square. Being found destitute and malnourished, she was returned to Lambeth Workhouse.

On being admitted yet again to Lambeth on 16 April 1888, a position of service was found for Polly the same day. She was to become a domestic servant to Samuel and Sarah Cowdray of Ingleside, Rose Hill Road, Wandsworth. The following day she sent a letter to her father, which read:

> 'I just write to say you will be glad to know that I am settled in my new place, and going all right up to now. My people went out yesterday and have not returned, so I am left in charge. It is a grand place inside, with trees and gardens back and front. All has been newly done up. They are teetotallers and religious so I ought to get on. They are very nice people, and I have not too much to do. I hope you are all right and the boy has work. So good bye for the present.
>
> From yours truly
>
> Polly
>
> Answer soon, please, and let me know how you are.'

Unfortunately, this brief interlude of stability was not to last, and in July 1888 she absconded, stealing clothing and money to the value of three pounds and ten shillings.

Mary Ann next appeared on 1 August at Gray's Inn Temporary Workhouse, where she remained overnight. From 2 August until 24 August she stayed at Wilmot's Lodging House at 18

Thrawl Street. While lodging there she became friendly with a fellow tenant named Ellen Holland. From 24 August Mary Ann was staying at 56 Flower and Dean Street, which was known locally as the White House. The building remained long after many of its neighbours were demolished and features in an iconic image of East End prostitutes sitting on the street, taken in 1901.

On the night of 30 August Nichols was seen at around 11pm, walking along Whitechapel Road. Ninety minutes later she was noticed leaving the Frying Pan public house in Brick Lane. The building can still be seen to this day. It is a very short distance up on the left and can easily be

Thrawl Street looking east, from *The People of the Abyss* by Jack London, 1902.

56 Flower and Dean Street (The White House), from *Living London* 1901.

The same arch as can be seen in the photo above, moved to its current location at the entrance to Flower and Dean Walk in the 1980s, photographed in 2004.

18 Thrawl Street was located approximately on the spot of the upright paving slab in this 2007 view.

identified by the original large terracotta plaque bearing the name of the old pub at the top corner of the building. She was next seen slightly inebriated at the lodging house at 18 Thrawl Street but, not having the money for a bed, the deputy turned her away. Mary Ann was laughing when she left and told the deputy 'I'll soon get my doss money; see what a jolly bonnet I've got now'. She was wearing a black straw bonnet, trimmed with black velvet, and had bought it only a few days previously. She felt the bonnet made her more attractive and thus was an aid to earning money.

At around 2.30am, Ellen Holland met Mary Ann at the junction of Osborn Street and Whitechapel Road, very close to where Emma Smith had been chased a few months

18 Thrawl Street, from *The Illustrated Police News*, 28 February 1891.

The Frying Pan public house, *c.*1930s. *(Courtesy Truman's Archive)*

The Frying Pan public house, 2007.

The junction of Whitechapel High Street and Osborn Street, 1890.

(Courtesy Tower Hamlets Local History Library and Archives)

The junction of Whitechapel High Street and Osborn Street, 2007.

previously. Holland was returning home after watching a fire at Shadwell Dry Dock. By this time, Nichols was very drunk and as a result Ellen tried to persuade her to return to 18 Thrawl Street. Nichols told Holland she had made her doss money three times over that day, but had spent it. After informing Holland she was now setting off to earn the money again, she proceeded east along Whitechapel Road. This was the last reported sighting of Polly Nichols alive.

Just over an hour later, at about 3.40am on the morning of 31 August 1888, Charles Cross (a carman employed by Pickfords of Broad Street) was passing through Buck's Row on his way to work, having left his home at 22 Doveton Street 10 minutes before. Cross was walking along the north side of the street, close to the façade of Brown & Eagle Ltd. The south side of Buck's Row, after the Roebuck Beer House on the eastern edge, consisted of a long terraced row of cottages constructed between 1862 and 1872. The last cottage to the west was called New Cottage, having been built in 1875 after some of the earlier cottages were demolished as the EastLondon Line was built underneath. The author Leonard Matters visited the street in 1928 and described it thus:

> 'It is a narrow, cobbled, mean street, having on one side the same houses - possibly tenanted by the same people - which stood there in 1888. They are shabby, dirty little houses of two stories, and only a three-foot pavement separates them from the road, which is no more than twenty feet from wall to wall.
>
> On the opposite sides are the high walls of warehouses which at night would shadow the dirty street in a far deeper gloom than its own character would in broad daylight suggest. All [the street] is not so drab and mean, for by some accident in the planning of the locality - if ever it was planned - quite two thirds of the thoroughfare is very wide and open'.

As he passed the end of the warehouses on the north Charles Cross noticed, on the other side of the road in front of the gates of Brown's Stable Yard, a shape he took to be a tarpaulin. Walking over to investigate he got as far as the middle of the road when he managed to ascertain it was actually a woman. In the few moments he considered what to do next, Cross heard footsteps from the same direction he had come. They belonged to Robert Paul of 30 Foster Street. Paul was also a carman but worked at nearby Corbett's Court off Hanbury Street. Cross stepped towards Paul and, tapping him on the shoulder said, 'Come over here; there's a woman lying on the pavement'. They approached the motionless woman with a degree of reticence. She was lying on her back, her skirt raised almost to her stomach. Cross touched her hand, which was cold and limp and commented 'I think she's dead'. He then touched her face, which was still warm. Robert Paul touched her heart and said 'I think she is breathing but it's very little if she is'. Both men decided

Durward Street (formerly Buck's Row), from *Jack the Ripper, A New Theory* by William Stewart, 1938.

Durward Street, 2007.

not to interfere further, but to inform the first policeman they encountered. However, before they left the scene, Robert Paul suggested propping the woman up but Cross refused, so Paul simply straightened the woman's skirt to give her some dignity and then both men made their way a short distance west towards Baker's Row.

PC John Neil 97J must have missed the presence of Cross and Paul at the gates by seconds. He turned into Buck's Row from Thomas Street (now called Fulbourne Street) at about 3.45am. It emerged about 50 yards west of the Board School; a huge square brick building constructed between 1876 and 1877. The building fell into dereliction and by the 1970s the threat of demolition hung over it, exacerbated by a fire in the early 1980s, although it was saved and turned into a block of luxury apartments in 1996. PC Neil walked down Buck's Row from the opposite direction to the two men. As he approached the stable gates he saw the woman for himself. Shining his light on her, he saw what the two men had missed in the darkness. Her throat had been cut twice: once from below the left ear extending to the middle of her neck; another starting a couple

The murder site was in front of the gates next to New Cottage, from *Jack the Ripper, A New Theory* by William Stewart, 1938.

A view from the opposite direction taken in the late 1960s. *(Courtesy J. E. Connor)*

The same view in 2006. The murder scene is by the shrubs in the middle of the picture.

of inches from the left ear and underneath the first cut, reaching across to the right ear. Blood was oozing from the wound. PC Neil felt the woman's right arm and it was quite warm from elbow upwards. As he was doing this he heard PC John Thain 96J passing the Brady Street end of Buck's Row, further to the east. Using his lamp, Neil signalled for Thain's assistance. Neil then sent Thain to fetch Dr Rees Ralph Llewellyn of 152 Whitechapel Road, which was near to the junction of Brady Street. His house no longer exists and a row of single-storey shops marks the area.

In the meantime, PC Neil crossed the street to Essex Wharf, a narrow three-storey building where he met Walter Purkiss, the night watchman for Brown & Eagle, and asked if he had heard anything. Neither Purkiss nor his wife – who was awake at the time – had heard a sound. Neil also knocked on the door of Mrs Emma Green, who lived in New Cottage next to the stable gates. Despite being a light sleeper she had also not heard anything. While PC Neil was talking to the local residents he was joined by PC Mizen 55H who had been approached by Charles Cross and Robert Paul at the junction of Baker's Row and Hanbury Street when they had told him what they had seen in Buck's Row. Neil sent Mizen to the Whitechapel Mortuary to fetch the police ambulance, which was actually nothing more than a covered handcart. The doctor arrived shortly after 4am and, after a very cursory examination, pronounced life extinct and ordered the body to be removed to the Whitechapel Mortuary, where only three weeks earlier Martha Tabram had been taken. At the time of Dr Llewellyn's arrival there were already several sightseers congregating around the body, including three men from Harrison, Barber & Co. Ltd, horse slaughterers from Winthrop Street (parallel to Buck's Row on the southern side of the Board School).

Inspector John Spratling of Bethnal Green Police Station was also sent for. He was in Hackney Road when he got news of the discovery of the body in Buck's Row. On reaching the spot, he found the deceased had already been removed to the mortuary, just a few short minutes walk further west. Making his way there he found the body lying on the cart outside the mortuary doors, as they were locked, although the keeper was being summoned. Inspector Spratling took down the woman's description: aged about 45, height 5ft 2in or 3in, complexion dark, hair dark brown (turning grey), eyes brown, bruise on the lower right jaw and left cheek, slight laceration of the tongue, one tooth deficient at the front of the upper jaw, two on the left of the lower jaw. Dress: brown ulster with seven large brass buttons with a figure of a female riding horse and a man at side thereon, brown linsey frock, grey woollen petticoat, flannel drawers, white chest flannel, brown stays, black ribbed woollen stockings, men's spring-sided boots (cut on the uppers and with tips on the heels), and a black straw bonnet (trimmed with black velvet).

Essex Wharf in 1989. The Purkiss's bedroom was at the front of the first floor.

Durward Street looking east (above), and west (below), from the murder site, September 1961.
(Courtesy Margaret Whitby-Green)

An ambulance cart similar to the one used to convey the victims of the Whitechapel Murderer to the mortuaries, from *Living London*, 1901.

The Whitechapel Mortuary. *(Courtesy Stewart P. Evans)*

On the arrival of the keeper, the body was swiftly moved into the mortuary itself, where Inspector Spratling made a more complete examination. It was while doing this that he noticed the woman had been partially disemboweled. At once, Inspector Spratling sent again for Dr Llewellyn, who returned to examine the remains more closely, and this examination was reported at the inquest.

On the right side of the face was a recently made and strongly marked

The approximate location of the Whitechapel Mortuary, 2007.

bruise, which was hardly noticeable when Llewellyn first saw the body. He thought that it could have been made by either a blow from a fist or by pressure of a thumb. On the left side of the face there was a circular bruise, which could have been caused in the same way. A small bruise was also apparent on the left side of the neck, and an abrasion was seen on the right. All of this must have been done at the same time. There were two cuts in the throat, one four inches long and the other eight, and both reaching to the vertebrae, which had also been penetrated. The wounds, he thought, must have been inflicted with a strong-bladed knife, moderately sharp, and used with great force. Dr Llewellyn believed a left-handed person made the incisions. There was no blood at all on the front of the woman's clothes. The body was fairly well nourished, and there was no smell of alcohol apparent in the stomach. On the abdomen were some severe cuts and stabs, which the witnesses described in detail, and some reports claim the intestines were protruding. Nearly all the blood had been drained out of the arteries and veins and collected to a large extent in the loose tissues and the back of the woman's clothing. Dr Llewellyn gave the opinion that the woman's wounds were sufficient to have caused instantaneous death.

A search was made of the vicinity around the scene of the crime, including the East London and District Railway and all the wharves and enclosures. The PC on duty at the Great Eastern Goods Yard was also questioned but he, like all the other people in the area, had not heard anything. Patrick Mulshaw (a night porter for the Whitechapel Board of Works) was watching the sewage works in Winthrop Street, which backed onto the rear of the Whitechapel Working Lads' Institute on Whitechapel Road. He said a man had passed him with the words 'I say, old man, a woman has been murdered up yonder'.

Buck's Row was in a different police division from the two earlier murders, which had occurred on H Division ground. It was in the jurisdiction of J Division, and this had only been formed two years earlier. The headquarters for J Division were in Bethnal Green Road. Local Inspector Joseph Helson headed the investigation into the Buck's Row murder, and to help him co-ordinate inquiries was Chief Inspector Frederick Abberline from Scotland Yard.

It wasn't long before the body was identified. Several women had already visited the mortuary to try and identify the remains but had failed to do so. The police soon discovered that a woman matching her appearance had been seen at the lodging house at 18 Thrawl Street. Ellen Holland

Winthrop Street looking east, c.1988.

Winthrop Street from Brady Street, 1910. *(Courtesy Tower Hamlets Local History Library and Archives)*

Bethnal Green Road, *c.1907*. The Police Station is the first building on the right.

was asked to try and identify the woman, whom she recognised as 'Polly'. There were markings on the deceased's clothing that denoted they belonged to the Lambeth Workhouse. As further corroboration, Mary Ann Monk (an inmate at that workhouse) identified the woman as that of Mary Ann Nichols and from this the police were then able to trace her relatives. Both her father, Edward Walker, and her estranged husband, William Nichols, identified her the next day on 1 September. William Nichols was visibly affected on viewing the body and is recorded as having said, 'I forgive you, as you are, for what you have been to me'. Her funeral was held on Thursday 6 September 1888 at the City of London Cemetery. Although buried in a common grave, which is now believed to lie under a roadway through the site, a memorial plaque has in recent years been set into the grass very close to the position of her burial.

Enquires into the murder of Mary Ann Nichols revealed that the police had no doubt that the murder was committed where the body was found and, despite extensive inquiries, Mary Ann Nichols's movements after she was seen by Ellen Holland could not be ascertained. The investigation did reveal that for some time the prostitutes of Whitechapel had been living in fear of a man who had been ill-treating them. He was a violent blackmailer who threatened to 'rip them up' if they did not meet his demands and was known by these prostitutes as 'Leather Apron'.

Little remains of Buck's Row today to give any indication of the claustrophobic atmosphere of 1888. The Board School still stands, and adjoining this is a length of original wall above the Tube train lines, which ends just before the murder spot. Next to this is a single remaining pillar of the gateway into a later garage that was built on the site of Brown's Stable Yard and was itself demolished in around 1966, though it was replaced with a more rigorous construction until about 1980. The exact area where Polly Nichols died was, in 2007, a small border of grass and shrubs around a few car-parking spaces. The murder spot is usually littered with refuse. The majority of the street came down during a period of regeneration in 1970–72, starting with the demolition of the warehouses on the northside in 1970. New Cottage, however, was one of the first places to be lost as a World War Two bomb blast destroyed it and the upper floors of many of the buildings in adjoining Winthrop Street. Most of the street remained an empty, desolate plot for nearly 20 years. Essex Wharf, a charming old building that was directly opposite the yard, was pulled down in 1990, followed by the Roebuck pub in 1995. A line of modern terraced houses named Kenton Court stands on the location of the Victorian cottages and most of Winthrop Street. On the north side stands a school and leisure centre.

Most importantly, Buck's Row itself technically no longer exists. Shortly after the Nichols murder, the council were successfully petitioned by the residents to change the name. As an example of the unwanted attention and notoriety their street had attained, residents spoke of

Scotland Yard, *c.*1880s.

their displeasure at the antics of one particular postman, who would knock on doors with letters and pass them over with phrases such as 'Number 1 Murder Row, I believe?'

On 25 October 1892 Buck's Row became Durward Street, the name it retains to this day.

ANNIE CHAPMAN

Annie Chapman was illegitimately born Annie Eliza Smith in September 1841 in Paddington, London, the first of five children born to George and Ruth Smith. On Saturday 1 May 1869 she married a Windsor coachman named John Chapman and they subsequently had three children together: Emily Ruth, Annie Georgina and John Alfred. Tragically, Emily Ruth Chapman died of meningitis on 26 November 1882, aged 12, and John Alfred was placed in an institution for physically disabled children because he was a cripple. Not long before Emily Ruth's death, Annie and John had separated and Annie went to live in London. The reason for the break-up is unclear, but it is alleged that Annie was a heavy drinker and was said to have walked the countryside like a common tramp. It was made clear to her that she was unwelcome at the family home. After a short stay in Windsor, Annie made her way to the slums of East London.

Mortuary photograph of Annie Chapman. *(Courtesy Stewart P. Evans)*

From this point until his death in Windsor on Christmas Day 1886, John Chapman made support payments to Annie of 10 shillings a week, although payment of this was often sporadic.

By 1886 Annie was living at a common lodging house located at 30 Dorset Street – just a few doors from Miller's Court, where the murder of Mary Jane Kelly would take place in November 1888. She began to co-habit with a sieve maker and was frequently referred to by the name Annie Siffey or Sievey, but the pair parted company early in 1887. As the only respectable way she had left to earn an income, Annie would often go to Stratford Market on Fridays to sell antimacassars, flowers and items of crochet work she had made. Prostitution was a last resort, but a role that was sometimes undertaken out of financial necessity.

At the time of her death in 1888, Annie Chapman was staying at 35 Dorset Street, a common lodging house about two-thirds of the way to the west on the north side of the street and on the corner with Little Paternoster Row, owned by William Crossingham. Crossingham owned several lodging houses in the district, including 17 Dorset Street and 8 White's Row. It was at 35 Dorset Street that she participated in a violent altercation with a fellow lodger named Eliza Cooper in late August 1888. The cause of the fight had been a bar of soap Annie had borrowed from her for an acquaintance, Ted Stanley. When Cooper asked for the return of the item later that day, she was affronted by Chapman's reply of 'I will see you by and by'. According to Timothy Donovan, the deputy of 35 Dorset Street, trouble flared again around 28 August in the kitchen of the lodging house. Eliza Cooper again asked for the return of the bar, at which Annie threw down a halfpenny onto a table and snapped, 'Go and get a halfpennyworth of soap'. The quarrel escalated and continued in the Britannia Beer House (commonly known as 'Ringers' by the locals, after the surname of the landlord) on the corner of the north side of Dorset Street and Commercial Street. Annie slapped Eliza in the face and she retaliated by punching Annie in the left eye and breast.

Crossingham's Lodging House, 35 Dorset Street, from *The Penny Illustrated Paper*, 8 June 1901.

On Monday 3 September Annie was seen by her friend Amelia Palmer in Dorset Street. Annie was by this stage sporting a black eye from her fight with Eliza Cooper and told Amelia she felt unwell. Amelia saw Annie again the next day outside Christchurch, Spitalfields, built by Nicholas Hawksmoor between 1714 and 1729 and remaining the most impressive building on the eastern side of Commercial Street. Again Annie complained of

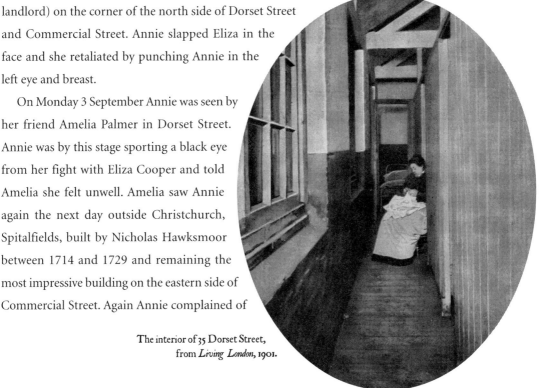

The interior of 35 Dorset Street, from *Living London*, 1901.

Commercial Street, c.1905.

feeling sick and told Amelia that she intended to go into the infirmary for a couple of days. Annie had not eaten or had anything to drink that day, so Amelia gave her tuppence for a cup of tea, with strict instructions not to spend it on rum, to which she knew Annie was very partial.

At about 5pm on 7 September, Amelia Palmer again met Annie in Dorset Street and enquired if she was going to travel to Stratford to do her usual street hawking. Annie replied 'I feel too ill to do anything'. About 10 minutes later, Amelia saw Annie again at the same spot. With more than a little pathos, Annie said, 'It's no use my giving way. I must pull myself together and go out and get some money, or I shall have no lodgings'. She clearly managed to summon some strength from somewhere, as a fellow lodger claimed she had made her way several miles to Vauxhall, where one of her sisters lived, and had been given fivepence. If this is true, it certainly didn't last long, as by the time she returned to 35 Dorset Street she was again penniless.

Around 11.30pm Annie went back into the lodging house and asked Timothy Donovan if she could sit in the kitchen. Donovan asked Annie where she had been all week and she replied she had indeed been in the infirmary.

Just before 2am on 8 September Annie was still in the kitchen at Crossingham's, eating potatoes. Timothy Donovan sent the night watchman John Evans to ask Annie for the money for her lodgings if she wished to remain in the building. She didn't have it, but asked Donovan not to let her bed go, as she would soon return with the price of her lodging. Annie left 35 Dorset Street and made her way north up Little Paternoster Row towards Brushfield Street, which runs parallel to the location of Dorset Street.

Hanbury Street in Spitalfields is just a couple of minutes walk further north up Commercial Street and starts on the eastern side, extending all the way down to Old Montague Street and Baker's Row (now Vallance Road) some distance to the south-east. Like a great many of the buildings in that area, many of the houses were constructed around the turn of the 18th century by the Huguenots, who were escaping persecution from the dominant Catholics in France. Many of the original houses still survive, especially in the evocative areas of Fournier Street (which was called Church Street in 1888), Wilkes Street and Princelet Street. As many of the Huguenots were silk weavers, a good many of the houses are identifiable by the large sash windows on the upper floors, designed to give maximum light by which the intricate work could be undertaken. 29 Hanbury Street stood almost exactly halfway between the junctions with Wilkes Street and Brick Lane, on the north side. It resembled many of the other terraced buildings along the street and in 1888 could certainly be classed as 'down at heel'. On the left side stood a shared dwelling, similar

29 Hanbury Street, September 1961. *(Courtesy Margaret Whitby-Green)*

in purpose to 29 itself, and on the other was a mangling house. The brick building had a cellar, reached from steps in the backyard. It was in this cellar that the owner of the building, Mrs Amelia Richardson, ran a packing-case business. She used two other rooms in the building as well but shared the front room on the first floor with her 14-year-old grandson. There was, at that time, a single entrance into the building on the left-hand side. Later photographs show two doorways from a time when access to the ground-floor shop became direct. In 1888, this one doorway led to another door directly on the right, which was a shop, fronted with large windows. This was where Harriet Hardiman worked and lived with her 16-year-old son, selling mostly horse meat to be fed to cats, though of course such cheap produce would on occasion be quietly bought for human consumption as well. A corridor leading off from the main front door led down to a staircase to the upper floors, at which point the corridor turned slightly to the right and continued down to the back door, hinged on the left. It then opened out onto two stone steps down into the back yard, which was about 15ft square with an outside lavatory in the top right corner. Next to Mrs Richardson's main room on the first floor was the room rented by Mr Walker, a maker of tennis boots, and his son. On the second floor were the three members of the Thompson family and two spinster sisters. Finally, in the attic there was a Mr John Davis (a carman), his wife and three sons and at the back lived Mrs Sarah Cox, who lived there free of charge thanks to Mrs

Hanbury Street looking east, January 1970. *(Courtesy Tower Hamlets Local History Library and Archives)*

Richardson's altruism. The residents in this one building totalled 17, and this was by no means considered overcrowded.

At 4.45am, John Richardson of 2 John Street, Spitalfields arrived and sat on the steps leading into the backyard to trim some leather from his boots. He was Amelia Richardson's son. While sitting on the steps in the early morning light he saw nothing untoward in the backyard and went on his way when he had done so.

Some time between 5.15 and 5.30am – certainly just after the brewery clock bell nearby had rung – Elizabeth Long (also known as Elizabeth Durrell) was approaching 29 Hanbury Street on her way to Spitalfields Market. She later claimed to have seen a man and woman standing by, or moving close to, the shutters in front of the shop. She later identified the woman, who was facing her, as Annie Chapman. The man, she claimed, was a little taller than the woman but she had been unable to see his face as he was wearing a deerstalker hat and was turned away from her,

Hanbury Street looking east, 2007.

facing Chapman. She did catch a short snippet of conversation as she passed the couple, which has passed into Ripper lore. The man, in a foreign accent, asked Annie a prophetic 'Will you?' to which Annie sealed her fate by replying 'Yes'. Given the events that followed, it is likely that Elizabeth Long had passed 29 Hanbury Street at about 5.20am, and not shortly after 5.30am as she remembered.

Albert Cadosch, who lived next door at number 27, went into his backyard at 5.25am. He heard two people talking in the backyard of number 29. The only word he caught was 'No.' He went back into the house and a few minutes later went again into the yard. This time he heard a gasp followed by a thud on the other side of the 5ft 6in temporary fence. Had he pulled himself up and looked over the top, he would almost certainly have been within inches of seeing the killer disposing of Annie Chapman. However, the use of the corridor and backyard at 29 Hanbury Street for prostitution was common, though disapproved of by residents, who often found themselves forcibly ejecting trespassers using the quiet and solitude for their nocturnal activities. Consequently, Cadosch didn't consider the noises on the other side of the fence to be out of the ordinary and went back into the building. Shortly afterwards, he left for work.

At around 6am, John Davis made his way down from the very top of 29 and went into the backyard. As he stood on the top step leading into the yard he saw, in the gap between the bottom of the door and the steps, and on the ground by the fence to his left, the body of Annie Chapman. Shocked by what he had discovered, he rushed out into Hanbury Street to look for help. There he met packing-case makers James Green and James Kent outside 23a Hanbury Street and a box maker named Henry John Holland, who was passing through Hanbury Street on his way to work. The three men went into the yard with John Davis and immediately dispersed to look for a

The interior of 29 Hanbury Street, looking from the front door, September 1961. *(Courtesy Margaret Whitby-Green)*

The interior of 29 Hanbury Street, looking from the back door, September **1961**. *(Courtesy Margaret Whitby-Green)*

policeman. The first to arrive on the scene was Inspector Joseph Chandler, who was found in Commercial Street. When Inspector Chandler arrived a crowd had already started to form around the entrance to number 29, but no one would enter the yard. The furore outside had caused Harriet Hardiman in the shop at the front to send her son to investigate. He returned with the words 'It's all right, mother – it's just another woman been murdered'! Annie Chapman's body was lying to the left of the bottom step, her head near to the back wall of the house. The injuries Annie received were more severe and extensive than those of Mary Ann Nichols and were described by Inspector Chandler:

> 'Left arm resting on left breast, legs drawn up, abducted small intestines and flap of the abdomen lying on right side, above right shoulder attached by a cord with the rest of the intestines inside the body; two flaps of skin from the lower part of the abdomen lying in a large quantity of blood above the left shoulder; throat cut deeply from left and back in a jagged manner right around the throat.'

On examining the immediate area of the yard around the body, he found six patches of blood varying in size about 18 inches from the ground, and smears of blood on the wooden fence about

The backyard of 29 Hanbury Street showing part of 27, September 1961. *(Courtesy Margaret Whitby-Green)*

Spital Square looking towards Folgate Street, September 1961. *(Courtesy Margaret Whitby-Green)*

14 inches from Annie's head. At Annie's feet were the contents of her pockets. Though they may have fallen out or been thrown out, some reports claim they were neatly arranged. These consisted of a small piece of course muslin, a small-tooth comb and a pocket comb in a paper case. Near Chapman's head was a piece of a torn envelope containing two pills. The back of the envelope had a seal and, embossed in blue, the words 'Sussex Regiment'. The front of the envelope contained the letter 'M' and underneath it 'Sp'. There was no postage stamp but a red postmark reading 'London, Aug 23, 1888'. It was eventually discovered that the envelope had been sent from the Lynchford Road Post Office in Farnborough, Hampshire, very close to the homes of several regiments of the British Army. This envelope turned out to be a red herring as William Stevens, a lodger at 35 Dorset Street, had seen Annie pick it up from the floor on the morning of her murder and wrap the pills in it. On the back wall of the house, hanging over a tap, was a leather apron. This too was

initially regarded as a clue, but was actually nothing more than the property of John Richardson. The apron had simply been washed and draped over the tap to dry.

Chandler sent for Dr George Bagster Phillips of 2 Spital Square (Spital Square is now largely part of the redevelopment of Spitalfields Market and is virtually unrecognisable. Phillips's house

1 and 2 Spital Square, 12 August 1908. *(Courtesy Brian Girling)*

Brushfield Street from Christ Church, Spitalfields, from *The People of the Abyss* by Jack London, 1902.

itself was demolished in 1929). Dr Phillips ordered the removal of the body to the Whitechapel Mortuary. Annie Chapman's body was quickly identified at 11.30am by her friend Amelia Palmer.

The house was searched and the inhabitants questioned, but not the slightest clue to the identity of the killer could be found. Tenants whose windows overlooked the backyard rented out window space to ghoulish sightseers to view the spot where the murder was committed. This could, perhaps, be deemed the first example of Ripper tourism, an educational leisure activity that seems to grow with each passing year.

An hour after John Davis discovered Annie Chapman's body, Mrs Fiddymont (the landlady of the Prince Albert in Brushfield Street) saw a strange man enter the pub. He so terrified her that she asked a friend, Mrs Mary Chappell of 28 Steward Street, to stay until he had gone. The man was described as wearing a stiff brown hat, drawn down to his eyes. His shirt was badly torn on the right shoulder and he had spots of blood on the back of his right hand, a narrow streak of blood under his right ear and dried blood between his fingers. He ordered a half-pint of ale, but when he noticed he was being observed from a distance by Mary Chappell, he turned his back to her, gulped down his drink and left.

Joseph Taylor followed him as far as Half Moon Street, Bishopsgate. This person was probably Jacob Isenschmid, a butcher of 59 Elthorne Road, Holloway. Several days later, on 11 September, a Dr Cowan and a Dr Crabb informed the police that they thought Isenschmid might well be the man responsible for the Whitechapel Murders. The police subsequently discovered that since 5 September he had been lodging with a Mr Tyler at 60 Milford Road. Isenschmid's whereabouts on the morning of the murder could not be accounted for and consequently he was detained on suspicion of murder on 12 September. Found to be mentally unsound, he was sent first to the workhouse and then to Fairfield Road Asylum, Bow. Sergeant Thick searched his clothing, but no traces of blood were found. Inspector Abberline believed him to be identical with the person seen by Mrs Fiddymont, but no identification could take place as Isenschmid's doctor would not allow it. It is clear the police at that time believed Isenschmid to be the leading suspect in Annie Chapman's murder, but any prospective culpability was soon forgotten when the later murders took place while he was safely confined within an asylum.

The inquest into the murder of Annie Chapman began on 10 September and continued for some days. This too was held at the Working Lads' Institute on Whitechapel Road.

She was buried on Friday 14 September 1888 at Manor Park Cemetery, Forest Gate, very close to where the train line from Liverpool Street passes by. Her body was collected at 7am from the

Mulberry Street, *c.*1940s.

Whitechapel Mortuary and taken, in a black-covered elm coffin, to Harry Hawes, a Spitalfields undertaker. The hearse set off at 9am and the ceremony was kept private with only relatives in attendance.

Today, Annie's grave is completely and irretrievably lost. The large plot in which she is buried has been lain with new bodies and memorials twice over.

The hunt for 'Leather Apron' increased. Timothy Donovan claimed to have ejected him from 35 Dorset Street once. Suspicion fell on John Pizer, a 38-year-old boot finisher who, it was said, was known by the nickname 'Leather Apron'. The reaction of the press was inflammatory and – whilst stopping short of giving his name – the physical description led to a witch-hunt against Pizer, who went into hiding. He was arrested at a relative's house at 22 Mulberry Street on 10 September. Mulberry Street stood on the north-west side of Commercial Road, although the street is no longer extant – the modern-day street that bears its name was called Union Row at the time and joined onto the north-western edge of the original Mulberry Street, which now lies largely under other buildings. Sergeant William Thick took Pizer to Leman Street Police Station. There, his whereabouts on the nights of 30–31 August and 7–8 September were rapidly ascertained. At the time of the Nichols murder, he had been outside a lodging house in Holloway Road, watching the distant dock fires. Two policemen and the lodging-house keeper confirmed his presence. For days before and after the Chapman murder, Pizer had been staying at the Mulberry Street address, too scared to leave because of the thinly veiled accusations cast in his direction. Although his innocence was clearly established, the public feeling against him was so strong that he appeared at the inquest on Annie Chapman on 11 September to publicly clear his name.

Another suspect was William Henry Piggott. He arrived in Gravesend at 4pm on 9 September, having apparently walked from Whitechapel. He left a paper parcel at a local fish shop and proceeded to arouse suspicion in the Pope's Head public house by expressing hatred towards women. The police were sent for and on their arrival Superintendent Berry noticed a wound to the back of his hand. Piggott claimed a woman had bitten him behind a Whitechapel lodging house. The parcel he left at the fish shop was searched and the police found a shirt with bloodstains on it. The police surgeon believed Piggott's shoes had been wiped clean of blood. Inspector Abberline took him back to Whitechapel, where an identity parade was held for Mrs Fiddymont, Joseph Taylor and Mary Chappell, but Fiddymont and Taylor failed to identify him. Mary Chappell picked him out but then retracted the assertion, saying she was no longer sure. Piggott's movements were accounted for and he was cleared of any involvement. Because of his unusual behaviour he was placed in the Whitechapel Union Infirmary by Sergeant Leach on 10 September and was discharged on 9 October 1888.

Two days after the Chapman murder, the Whitechapel Vigilance Committee was formed in

The Crown Public House, Mile End Road, a little east of the murder locations but still within the locale. George Lusk of 1 Tollet Street, Alderney Road, Stepney Green was elected president of the Vigilance Committee. His house still stands to this day. The purpose of this group was to attempt to help the investigation and to keep watch for suspicious behaviour in the hope of catching the killer.

On 25 September Sir Charles Warren, Metropolitan Police Commissioner, received the first letter allegedly from the killer:

> Sep 24 1888
>
> Dear sir
>
> I do wish to give myself up I am in misery with nightmare I am the man who committed all these murders in the last six months my name is so and so [silhouette of a coffin] I am a horse slauterer and work at name [blacked out] address [blacked out] I have found the woman I wanted that is chapman and I done what I called slautered her but if any one comes I will surrender but I am not going to walk to the station by myself so I am yours truly [partial silhouette of a coffin] keep the Boro road clear or I might make a trip up there photo of knife [here was placed a cartoon of a knife] this is the knife that I done these murders with it is a small handle with a long blade sharpe both sides

In recent years a letter has also been discovered dated 17 September, one week earlier. However, analysis and expert detective work have shown that this is almost certainly a forgery, dating from later than 1966.

From mild beginnings, the floodgates opened and on 27 September the Central News Agency, 5 New Bridge Street, received the notorious 'Dear Boss' letter. This letter is without doubt the most famous artefact connected with the Ripper crimes as it is the source of the term 'Jack the Ripper'. The building that housed the Central News Agency still exists on a very busy street close to Ludgate Circus. Although to this day some people believe the letter was written by the killer himself, it was probably the creation of two journalists named Charles Moore and Tom Bulling. The Central News Agency provided stories to the London newspapers and it is highly unlikely the killer would have known about it and contacted them directly. Moore and Bulling worked for the Central News Agency and probably concocted the letter to keep the story in the public eye and also to earn a little money by selling the story to the London press. In fact, it is highly unlikely that any of the avalanche of taunting letters received by the police and press over the coming months and years had any genuine provenance.

The text of the 'Dear Boss' letter reads as follows:

Dear Boss

I keep on hearing the police have caught me but they wont fix me just yet. I have laughed when they look so clever and talk about being on the right track. That joke about Leather Apron gave me real fits. I am down on whores and shant quit ripping them till I do get buckled. Grand work the last job was. I gave the lady no time to squeal. How can they catch me now. I love my work and want to start again. You will soon hear of me with my funny little games. I saved some of the proper <u>red</u> stuff in a ginger beer bottle over the last job to write with but it went thick like glue and I can't use it. Red ink is fit enough I hope <u>ha.ha.</u> The next job I do I shall clip the lady's ears off and send to the police officers just for jolly wouldn't you. Keep this letter back till I do a bit more work. then give it out straight. My knife's so nice and sharp I want to get to work right away if I get a chance. Good luck.

Yours truly

Jack the Ripper

Don't mind me giving the trade name

Wasn't good enough to post this before I got all the red ink off my hands curse it. No luck yet.

They say I'm a doctor now <u>ha ha</u>

New Bridge Street, 1895.

The Central News Agency (where the railings begin), 2007.

In spite of the dubious origins of this letter, several days later the real killer did kill again, and a coincidental knife cut through a victim's right ear lobe made people feel that perhaps this taunting and oddly-phrased letter had truly come from a killer who was now calling himself Jack the Ripper.

29 Hanbury Street can still be seen today, but only on film. James Mason briefly visited the location when hosting the excellent travelogue *The London Nobody Knows* in 1967. By that time, many of the houses on the northern side were unoccupied. Hanbury Street has undergone changes, but these did not take place until the early 1970s. Although the southern side of that section of the street remains untouched, with the exception of some garish coats of paint and numerous illuminated signs outside the businesses that trade there, the northern side has completely vanished. It was replaced with an extremely unappealing modern brewery building, with blank brick walls and shallow metal gables running the length from Wilkes Street to Brick Lane. The brewery itself has now moved elsewhere and the shell of the building now serves as a

covered car park and weekend marketplace. The spot where Annie Chapman died would now be totally undetectable were it not for satellite mapping. It is on the internal roadway between two sets of parking bays and a pair of concrete pillars.

SUSAN WARD

Little is known of the attack on Susan Ward and the crime is often no more than a footnote. However, there is a possibility that this woman was indeed a 'lucky' survivor of a Ripper maiming. Although the date is usually referred to as being around 15 September, it could in fact have been any time between 8 and 23 September. The only contemporary report states the attack took place somewhere around Commercial Street, which presents a very large area. Some modern accounts erroneously refer to Commercial Road instead. From the Susan Wards found on the 1891 Census, it is likely she came from Bethnal Green, but even this cannot be confirmed.

The Daily Telegraph reported on 3 October 1888 that 'about ten days previously' a woman had been admitted to London Hospital suffering from a knife wound inflicted during an unprovoked attack in the street. Part of the newspaper's report reads:

> An alarming story was told to a detective yesterday, and it is understood that the Metropolitan police have for some time been cognisant of its details. If this statement be true, and there appears to be no reason to question it, then some time between the date of the Hanbury-street murder and last Sunday the bloodthirsty maniac who is now terrifying Whitechapel unsuccessfully attempted another outrage. The woman who so narrowly escaped death is married, but she admits having entered into conversation with a strange man for an immoral purpose. She alleges that he tripped her up, so that she fell upon the pavement. He made an effort to cut her throat, but she shielded herself with her arm, and in so doing received a cut upon it. Alarmed by his failure, and fearing her shrieks, the would-be murderer ran off, and the woman, when discovered, was removed to the hospital. She has since been discharged, and the wound upon the arm is still to be seen. The occurrence is alleged to have taken place ten days ago, in a bye-turning off Commercial-street. Unfortunately the woman was so much in liquor when she was assaulted that she cannot recollect the man's face or dress, and has been unable to give a description of him, which may account for the secrecy which has been maintained in regard to the attack.

The item goes so far as to say it occurred in a 'bye-turning', which would present countless locations. The only woman treated for knife wounds at the London Hospital around that time was

Commercial Street, 1912.

Susan Ward, who had actually been admitted on 15 September. Some reports claim the wound on her arm did not appear to be very recent. The fact this woman was drunk, accepted an indecent proposition and then saved herself from having her throat cut does make it likely that – if her story was true – she had just prevented herself from becoming another victim of the Ripper.

ELIZABETH STRIDE

On Monday 27 November 1842, Elisabeth Gustafsdotter was born to the farmer Gustaf Ericsson and his wife Beata Carlsdotter in a farm called Stora Tumlehed in Torslanda, Sweden. She was the second of four children. On 25 October 1860, she moved to the nearby city of Gothenburg and a few months later, in February 1861, she found herself in the employ of Lars-Fredrik Olofsson, working as a domestic servant. She left the position almost

Mortuary photograph of Elizabeth Stride. *(Courtesy Stewart P. Evans)*

79

exactly three years later and it was about this time that she drifted into prostitution to make ends meet. It wasn't long before this became her main source of income and she officially registered as a prostitute in March 1865. By this time she was heavily pregnant and on 21 April she gave birth to a stillborn baby girl. Due to a change of heart, or perhaps a change of fortune, Elisabeth was struck from the prostitutes' register before the end of the year and on 14 November she began a job as a servant to a woman named Inga Maria Wenzel.

In either December 1864 or March 1866, Elisabeth received an inheritance of 65 Crowns from her mother, who had died in 1864. This was, at that time, a considerable sum and she used it to emigrate to England. English posed little problem to her as she spoke four languages fairly fluently. She arrived in London on 7 February 1866. On 10 July that year she registered as an unmarried woman at the Swedish Church in Prince's Square, St George's in the East, between Cable Street and the Ratcliffe Highway. By this time it had been renamed St George Street, but this had hardly erased the memory of the notorious mass murders that had taken place there at the hand of John Williams earlier in the century. The first Swedish congregation in London had been formed in 1710 and the church here was completed in 1727. It closed in 1911 and today a modern housing

The interior of the Swedish Church, from *Living London*, 1901.

The site of the Swedish Church, 2006.

estate with high-rise flats stands in its place. The road running through it is named Swedenborg Gardens, not after the church, but after the philosopher and scientist Emmanuel Swedenborg who was buried in the crypt (his remains being moved three years before the church closed). The original church font is still on display in the open air where the church stood and is sadly much vandalised.

On 7 March 1869 Elisabeth married John Thomas Stride at St Giles-in-the-Fields church in Holborn. The church still exists, very close to the busy intersection of Oxford Street and Charing Cross Road and dwarfed by Centre Point, which stands close by. At the time of the marriage, Elizabeth (having now Anglicised her name) was living at 67 Gower Street close to Euston Square. This building also still stands, now absorbed into the hotel next door. It is a large terraced town house built, like much of Gower Street, in the early 1800s.

After the marriage, the pair moved east and kept a coffee shop in Chrisp Street, Poplar. In 1870 they moved their business to Upper North Street and later to 178 East India Dock Road. In 1875 the business was taken over by a John Dale. John and Elizabeth separated in around 1877. In later

St Giles in the Fields Church, 2007.

years, Liz was to tell acquaintances that her husband – and children, of which there is no evidence – had been drowned in the *Princess Alice* disaster on 3 September 1878. This event has now been largely forgotten, but remains the most serious inland shipping loss in England. The *Princess Alice* was a pleasure steamer and on the day in question was severely overloaded. The *Bywell Castle* was a collier six times her size and late in the evening the bow of the larger ship ploughed into the cruiser, sending her to the bottom in just five minutes at Galleon's Reach in Woolwich, with an unconfirmed mortality rate of about 700 and just 50 survivors. Liz was also

67 Gower Street, 2007.

to claim she now suffered from a mouth deformity caused by being kicked in the face while she was struggling to save herself from the sinking ship. This was, of course, total fantasy.

Between 28 December 1881 and 4 January 1882 Liz was treated at the Whitechapel Union Infirmary, Baker's Row for bronchitis. She was then sent to the Whitechapel Workhouse, South Grove, for three days. When she left the Workhouse she began to lodge on and off at a common lodging house at 32 Flower and Dean Street. This building was on the north side of the street, close to the junction with Commercial Street. The location of the old building now lies under a multi-purpose sports court at the end of the very short road called Lolesworth Close, which is all that remains of this infamous street.

John Stride died at Poplar Workhouse on 24 October 1884 and, probably early the following year, Liz met a dockside labourer by the name of Michael Kidney. They took up residence at 35 Devonshire Street, just off Commercial Road and very close to Star Place, where Martha Tabram once lived. They moved to 36, next door, five months before Liz died. At the time of Liz's murder, Kidney was to give his address as 38 Dorset Street. By this time, Elizabeth was also known by the

Chrisp Street Market, Poplar, 1906.

East India Dock Road, **1912.** Upper North Street is on the extreme left.

nickname 'Long Liz', and some have attempted to explain this by saying she was a very tall woman. She was actually of just above average height and the prefix 'Long' was a frequent tongue-in-cheek name given to those with the surname Stride (as in long strides).

On 20 and 23 May 1886 Liz received alms from the Swedish Church. She gave the Devonshire Street address and the clerk, Sven Olsson, described her as 'very poor'. On 21 March 1887 she registered as an inmate at Poplar Workhouse. The following month she accused Kidney of assault, but the case was dismissed when she failed to attend at Thames Magistrates Court.

Charles Preston, a barber who had lodged at 32 Flower and Dean Street for 18 months, was later to

Poplar Workhouse, from *The People of the Abyss* by Jack London, **1902.**

report that in the early summer of 1888 Liz had been arrested for being drunk and disorderly at the Queen's Head public house in Commercial Street. In the 20 months prior to her death she had appeared before the magistrate on eight occasions facing similar charges.

The Swedish Church again found themselves granting Liz Stride charity on 15 and 20 September 1888. Five days later, on Tuesday 25, Michael Kidney saw Liz Stride for the last time in Commercial Street. The following day, Liz turned up at 32 Flower and Dean Street. She mentioned to a long-time acquaintance called Catherine Lane, a charwoman who lived there with her husband, that she had 'had words' with the man she was living with. It is likely that later that day she was one of the women who met the social philanthropist Dr

32 Flower and Dean Street, from *Famous Crimes Past and Present*, edited by Harold Furniss, 1903.

Lolesworth Close, 2007. 32 Flower and Dean Street stood just past the iron gates, on the left hand side.

Thomas Barnardo in the kitchen of 32. On 6 October, Barnardo wrote a letter to The Times, which was published three days later:

> 'The pathetic part of my story is that my remarks were manifestly followed with deep interest by all the women. Not a single scoffing voice was raised in ridicule or opposition. One poor creature, who had evidently been drinking, exclaimed somewhat bitterly to the following effect: 'We're all up to no good, and no one cares what becomes of us. Perhaps some of us will be killed next!' and then she added, 'If anybody had helped the likes of us long ago we would never have come to this!'
>
> Impressed by the unusual manner of the people, I could not help noticing their appearance somewhat closely, and I saw how evidently some of them were moved. I have since visited the mortuary in which were lying the remains of the poor woman Stride, and I at once recognised her as one of those who stood around me in the kitchen of the common lodging-house on the occasion of my visit last Wednesday week.

On Saturday 29 September, Liz spent the afternoon cleaning two rooms in the lodging house, for which she was paid sixpence by the deputy, Elizabeth Tanner. Tanner was to see Stride in the

The Bricklayer's Arms, Settles Street, 2007.

Commercial Road from Gardiner's Corner, *c.*1930. (Courtesy Tower Hamlets Local History Library and Archives)

nearby Queen's Head at 6.30pm and, after having a drink together, they both returned to 32 Flower and Dean Street. Between 7pm and 8pm Liz left the lodging house and was seen as she departed by both Charles Preston and Catherine Lane. She gave Lane a large piece of green velvet, which she asked her to keep until she returned. She asked to borrow Preston's clothes brush, but he had mislaid it. As she left, she passed the watchman of 32, a man named Thomas Bates. He was later to report that she had appeared cheerful.

At 11pm, two labourers (J. Best of 82 Lower Chapman Street and John Gardner of 11 Chapman Street) were entering the Bricklayer's Arms pub on Settles Street, at its junction with Fordham Street and just north of Commercial Road. This building has managed to survive, but is now used as a supermarket, an exterior trapdoor close to the wall giving away its former purpose. As the labourers were entering, they saw Stride leaving with a short man who had a dark moustache and sandy eyelashes. The man was wearing a billycock hat (a type of bowler hat), morning suit and a coat. Best later said, 'They had been served in the public house and went out when me and my friends came in. It was raining very fast and they did not appear willing to go out. He was hugging and kissing her, and as he seemed a respectably dressed man, we were rather astonished at the way he was going on at the woman'.

Liz and the man remained in the doorway for some time, still engaged in their passionate intentions. The workmen made attempts to get the well-dressed man back into the pub, but he refused to join them. They jeered to her, 'That's Leather Apron getting round you'. Shortly after 11pm, she and her companion left quickly in the direction of Commercial Road and Berner Street, in Best's words, 'like a shot'.

At 11.45pm, William Marshall, a labourer, saw Liz Stride in Berner Street, running south from Commercial Road. He was standing in the doorway of 64, on the west of the street between Fairclough Street and Boyd Street, and observed Liz Stride and a man outside 63, behaving in a similar manner to that reported by the men in the Bricklayer's Arms. This may have been a different man, however, as Marshall claimed he had been wearing a short cutaway coat and a sailor's hat. Marshall heard him say to Liz, 'You would say anything but your prayers'.

Berner Street was named on 1 May 1868, an amalgamation of Upper and Lower Berner Streets and Batty Buildings. It was named Henriques Street in 1964 after Basil Henriques OBE, who founded a youth club named the Bernhard Baron Oxford and St George Settlement in 1914. The

Berner Street looking towards Ellen Street in 1938. Elizabeth Stride was seen near the lam-post by William Marshall. *(Courtesy Tower Hamlets Local History Library and Archives)*

Berner Street showing the entrance to Dutfield's Yard, 7 April 1909.

Berner Street, 2007.

street was regarded as respectable in the 1880s and had a fair mix of businesses, shops, pubs and houses.

At midnight, Matthew Packer (who sold fruit from his address at 44 Berner Street) claimed to have sold half a pound of black grapes to a man with Liz Stride. He watched the pair cross the road and stand in the rain. Half an hour later, he decided to close up for the night. Packer's testimony has often been disputed and there are those who think he might have been mistaken or just trying to get his name in the papers by claiming to be a witness. This was a frequent problem, and even to this day much of what is 'known' of the Whitechapel Murders could be nothing more than the surviving inventions of creative and attention-seeking minds.

At around 12.30am, a printer and photographer called Joseph Lave left the International Workers' Educational Club on the north side of Dutfield's Yard at 40 Berner Street to get some fresh air and noticed how quiet the street seemed. He went back into the building at 12.40am, about the time Morris Eagle was entering (seeing nothing untoward) through the side entrance. There are no surviving photographs of the interior of Dutfield's Yard and only a handful of contemporary sketches. The only known photograph of the entrance to the yard has been reproduced countless times and was taken on 7 April 1909, shortly before this side of the street was demolished and redeveloped.

Dutfield's Yard itself was described in *The Star* on 1 October 1888:

> The scene of the murder was within the gateway at No. 40, which is occupied by a Jewish working men's club under the name of the International Men's Educational Society. It is a building of two stories. A passage wide enough to admit a cart separates it from the next house... There is an entrance to the club from the street, and also one from the court. The court is very small. The club building occupies one side and three dwelling-houses the other, and there are premises belonging to Walter H. Hindley and Co, sack manufacturers, and Arthur Dutfield, van and cart builder, at the further end of the court. At night this courtyard is dark except for the light from the house windows. At the street entrance there is a large folding door, on the right half of which there is a small panel door. The large gate is supposed to be shut every night, but the small door is left open for the use of persons living in the court... Besides the club, there are three dwelling houses in the court...

Mrs Fanny Mortimer of 36 Berner Street was standing in the doorway of her house for half an hour from 12.30am. She saw a couple at the corner of Berner Street and Fairclough Street by the Board School. Mrs Mortimer spoke to them after the murder had taken place and this may therefore be the couple seen by another witness, James Brown.

At 12.35am, PC William Smith 452H saw Liz with a young man on the opposite side of the street to the entrance to Dutfield's Yard. The club there was a pseudo-socialist/anarchist club for men from Eastern Europe and was looked upon with some distrust by the locals. On the night in question, there had been a lecture on the subject of 'Why Jews should be Socialists', followed by leisure activities and singing. The music could be heard from the street and it is possible the couple were listening to it. PC Smith noticed Liz was wearing a red rose. He described the man as

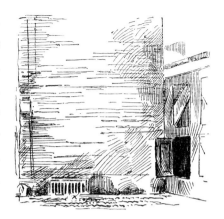

Dutfield's Yard, from *The Weekly Dispatch*, 7 October 1888.

approximately 28 years of age and 5f 7in tall. He was wearing a dark coat and a hard deerstalker hat. He was also carrying a parcel wrapped in newspaper about six inches high and 18 inches long.

Israel Schwartz of 22 Ellen Street (which ran across the bottom end of Berner Street) was

The site of Dutfield's Yard, 2007. *(Courtesy Colin Roberts)*

Berner Street looking towards Batty Gardens, 7 April 1909.

walking down the street from Commercial Road. When he got as far as Dutfield's Yard, he saw a man stop and speak to a woman who was standing in the gateway. The man tried to pull her into the street but she would not move and he turned her round, throwing her onto the ground. She screamed three times, but not very loudly. As Schwartz crossed the street to keep his distance, he noticed a man outside the Nelson Beer House a few doors down, smoking a pipe in the doorway. Liz's assailant looked up and called out 'Lipski!' in their direction. This was a colloquial term of insult towards Jews at that time, following the murder of Miriam Angel by a Jew named Israel Lipski in Batty Street, just one street to the east of Berner Street, the previous year. Whether this was some kind of instruction to the man in the doorway and just who it was directed towards, we will never know. Schwartz claimed the man in the doorway began to follow him and, concerned he was about to be beaten himself, he began to run south as far as the railway arches, but the man from the doorway did not go that far. Schwartz was unable to say if the man in the doorway was known to the man attacking Liz, but some have theorised that his account provides evidence for the Ripper having had an accomplice.

Schwartz was later to identify Liz Stride's body in St George's in the East Mortuary as the woman he had seen being assaulted. He was able to describe the man attacking Liz as about 30 years old, 5ft 5in tall with a fresh complexion, dark hair and a small brown moustache. He was dressed in an overcoat with an old black felt hat which had a wide brim.

At around the same time, James Brown said he had seen Liz with a man as he was returning home with his supper walking down Fairclough Street, which ran east to west and bisected Berner Street. She was leaning against the wall of the Board School opposite and talking to a man of stocky build, 5ft 7in tall, wearing a long black coat which almost touched the ground. He had his arm against the wall. Brown heard the woman say 'No, not tonight. Maybe some other night'.

At 1am, Louis Diemschutz, the steward at the club in Dutfield's Yard, was returning home with his pony and cart from a day's work selling cheap costume jewellery at Westow Hill, Sydenham. As he turned off Commercial Road and down into Berner Street he noticed the clock in the window of Harris's Tobacconists showing the time as exactly one o'clock. The building still exists today, at the junction of Henriques Street and Commercial Street on the eastern side. There was no fog that night – in fact, there was no fog on the night of any Ripper murder – but it was very windy, and it was raining. Diemschutz pulled the cart onto the right-hand side and into the open gateway of Dutfield's Yard but the pony whinnied, shied away to the left, and refused to proceed further. The driver poked about with his whip and came into contact with an object that should not have been there. He struck a match to see more clearly and, in the few moments before the wind blew it out, he was able to see what had so disturbed the pony. Diemschutz was just able to make out a woman lying with her head facing the far end of the yard, against the right-hand wall, her feet almost touching the open gateway. His first thought was that the woman was his wife and that she was drunk.

He went into the club to get some help in waking the woman and, when he returned with

100 Commercial Road from *The Illustrated Police News*, 9 July 1887.

Harris's Tobacco Shop, Commercial Road, *c.*1905.

Isaac Kozebrodsky and Morris Eagle, the three discovered that the woman was dead and her throat was cut. She had only recently been killed and blood was still seeping from the wound and slowly trickling down the yard. They ran to find a policeman and quickly met PC Lamb 252H, who went to the spot and summoned Dr George Bagster Phillips from Spital Square, some distance north, and Dr Frederick William Blackwell of 100 Commercial Road (very close by, at the junction with Batty Street).

The woman was 5ft 5in tall, with a pale complexion, grey eyes and long curly brown hair. All the teeth had long been missing from her lower jaw.

The position of the body and the injuries were recorded as follows:

> The body was lying on the near side, with the face turned toward the wall, the head up the yard and the feet toward the street. The left arm was extended and there was a packet of cachous [breath-sweetening confections] in the left hand.

> The right arm was over the belly; the back of the hand and wrist had on it clotted blood. The legs were drawn up with the feet close to the wall. The body and face were warm and the hand cold. The legs were quite warm.

> Deceased had a silk handkerchief round her neck, and it appeared to be slightly torn. I have since ascertained it as cut. This corresponded with the right angle of the jaw. The throat was deeply gashed and there was an abrasion of the skin about one and a half inches in diameter, apparently stained with blood, under her right arm.

The body was removed to St George's in the East Mortuary. The structure still stands, albeit as a secluded ruin. Its location was only discovered in recent years. It lies in the graveyard of St George's Church in Cannon Street Road, Shadwell. The church itself was built in 1729 by Hawksmoor but was internally destroyed in the Blitz and was restored in 1966, and it is just across from the church where Joseph Martin lived at 11 Cannon Street Road. Martin was the man responsible for taking some of the photographs of the Ripper victims. The mortuary behind the church was the second mortuary in the graveyard and was built around 1876. It is a small brick building entered through a porch on the north side, leading through a small vestibule into the mortuary itself. The vestibule area is covered in white tiles and there is a small wooden cupola on what remains of the roof, but these may date from the early 20th century when it was turned into a nature study centre. A large fragment of roof truss remains outside the building and the surviving glass in the three very narrow lancet windows on the eastern end of the mortuary area itself is half an inch thick. The building is very secure and it is difficult to see through the gaps

St George's in the East Mortuary, 2007.

The jury leaving St George's in the East Mortuary, from *The Pictorial News*, 16 October 1888.

between the sheets of corrugated iron that block all the apertures. In recent years there have even been plans submitted to convert the building into a small house.

Just outside the graveyard is the Vestry Hall (now more commonly named Stepney Town Hall), on the south side of Cable Street and very close to Shadwell tube station. This is where the inquest was held.

There was difficulty in identifying the body held in the mortuary. Mrs Mary Malcolm of 50 Eagle Street, Red Lion Square, Holborn, came forward on 1 October and identified the dead woman as

The interior of St George's in the East Mortuary, 2006.

her estranged sister, Elizabeth Watts. Malcolm had claimed to have had a premonition at 1.20am the previous morning, shortly after Liz Stride's body was found. She was sure something had happened to her sister and when lying in bed she felt a pressure on her breast and then felt – and heard – three kisses on her cheek. However, such confidence was misplaced when the real Elizabeth Watts – by now named Elizabeth Stokes – let it be known that she was still very much alive.

The interior of St George's in the East Mortuary, from *The Penny Illustrated Paper*, 6 October 1888.

The Vestry Hall, Cable Street, 1906.

The Vestry Hall, Cable Street, 2007.

The burial site of Elizabeth Stride, 2007.

On the morning of 1 October, at about half-past midnight, Thomas Coram found a bloodstained knife about 9–10 inches long on the steps of 252 Whitechapel Road, on the south side between Vine Court (the site of the notorious Wainwright murder a little over a decade previously) and Fieldgate Street, where the ancient Whitechapel Bell Foundry still stands. There was a bloodstained handkerchief wrapped around it and the knife was produced at the inquest on Elizabeth Stride, but Dr Phillips was of the opinion that such a knife was unlikely to have been the cause of the throat wound.

Eventually the body was identified by Michael Kidney and official identification was given by PC Walter Stride, Liz's nephew through marriage. Elizabeth was buried without great cost or ceremony at the East London Cemetery in Plaistow on Saturday 6 October 1888. In recent years, a tasteful concrete surround and headstone have been erected above the rough position of her final resting place.

Today, the playground of the Harry Gosling Primary School innocently stands over Dutfield's Yard and the place where Elizabeth Stride died.

CATHERINE EDDOWES

Catherine Eddowes was born to a tin plate worker named George and his wife Catherine on 14 April 1842 at Graisley Green in Wolverhampton, West Midlands. She was the sixth of twelve children at a time when it was not unusual to have a large family due to the expectation of losing some through the high rate of infant mortality in impoverished areas. In 1843 the family walked down to London to relocate. Catherine was orphaned at the age of 14; her mother died in 1855 and her father two years later. It was about the time her father passed away that she returned to Wolverhampton and got a job as a scourer. At that time she was recorded as living at 50 Bilston Street.

In 1862, Catherine was found stealing from her employers and ran away to live with an uncle, Thomas Eddowes at the Brick Hill, Bagot Street, Birmingham. She began work in the city as a tray polisher in Legge Street. After a brief period here she returned to Wolverhampton again to live with her grandfather (also Thomas). She moved herself to Birmingham one more time and it was then that she met Thomas Conway, a street hawker. Conway had a low but steady income as he was drawing an army pension, having once been a soldier. They lived a nomadic existence, moving from town to town selling chapbooks written by Conway. Catherine had his initials, TC, tattooed in blue ink on her forearm and although they claimed to be married, a ceremony had never taken place.

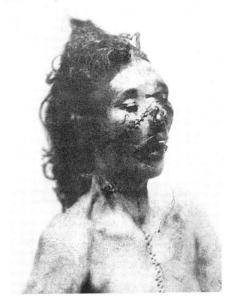

Mortuary photograph of Catherine Eddowes. *(Courtesy Stewart P. Evans)*

Conway and Eddowes had three children together: Ann (born 18 April 1863 at Yarmouth Workhouse), Thomas (born 1868) and Alfred George (born 15 August 1873). Catherine was calling herself Catherine Conway at this time.

By 1881 the family were living at 71 Lower George Street in Chelsea. This residency was to be short-lived as later that year the couple finally separated. Thomas cited Catherine's heavy drinking, which had begun in the 1860s, and she in turn stated that he used to beat her. On parting, Catherine moved to Spitalfields, the area where her sister, Eliza Gold, had lived for some years.

Shortly after arriving in Spitalfields, Catherine began living with John Kelly. They were to remain together, mostly staying at Cooney's lodging house at 55 Flower and Dean Street, for the rest of Catherine's life. This lodging house was next door to the White House, on the north side of the street. The lodgers at Cooney's knew Catherine as Mrs Kelly, although she would also name herself Catherine Conway.

Before the year was out, Catherine appeared at Thames Police Court on 21 September for being drunk and disorderly and using obscene language. She was discharged without a fine.

Flower and Dean Street, 2007. The approximate location of 55 and 56 is where the road starts to curve.

Flower and Dean Street from Brick Lane, from *The Mystery of Jack the Ripper* by Leonard Matters, 1928.

In 1886 Catherine attended the confinement of her daughter, Ann, who gave birth to her third child. It was at this time that Ann told Catherine she wanted nothing further to do with her. The reason given was that Catherine only appeared to be interested in getting money from her relatives. Thomas Conway had kept the whereabouts of their two sons a secret for the same reason.

On 14 June 1887, Catherine was admitted to the Whitechapel Union Infirmary, having somehow suffered a burn on her foot. She was discharged six days later.

In early September 1888, Catherine and John Kelly made the journey south-east to Hunton, near Coxheath in Kent, to go hop picking. 'Hopping' was a regular excursion for the London poor well into the middle of the 20th century. It served a two-fold benefit: of being a type of family holiday, and of earning money to see the way into the coming winter months. At Maidstone, Catherine bought a pair of boots from a shop in the High Street run by Arthur Pash. She also obtained a jacket from a pawnbroker's shop run by a Mr Edmett. Whilst still in Kent, she was given a pawn ticket by a woman named Emily Birrell to collect a man's shirt from a London pawnbroker. Birrell was moving to Cheltenham in Gloucestershire, so would not be returning to collect it.

Joseph Jones Pawnbrokers, 3 Fournier Street (formerly 31 Church Street), 2007.

Unfortunately, the season had been a bad one and the wages had been low. Catherine and John cut their losses and walked back to London, arriving on 27 September. That night, they spent the night in the casual ward at the workhouse at Shoe Lane. The following day, John managed to secure some work and was paid sixpence for it. This was, however, not enough to pay for a double room at Cooney's, so Catherine insisted he take fourpence for a bed and she spent her last full night alive in the casual ward at Mile End.

At 8am the following morning, Catherine went to Cooney's and met John. They agreed to pawn the boots John had bought at the pawnbroker's run by Joseph Jones at 31 Church Street. Church Street was renamed Fournier Street on 7 November 1893 and has also been renumbered. Fournier Street, like Hanbury Street, features in the film *The London Nobody Knows* and again contains two rows of terraced town houses built by the Huguenots. The street is best known today for being the home of the controversial artists Gilbert & George. Hawksmoor's church stands on Commercial Street at the south-western end, and the famous Ten Bells pub stands opposite at the north-western end. At the east, the street joins on to Brick Lane. Many of the buildings still have interesting old porches. Jones' pawnbrokers at 31 Church Street is now 3 Fournier Street, two doors down from the Ten Bells. Recently, even an early Jones banner over the shop window, *c.*1900, has been restored. Catherine and John were given 2s 6d for the boots, and with this they bought tea and sugar and were able to have some breakfast at Cooney's.

They spent the rest of the morning together but finally parted company in Houndsditch, within the square mile of the City of London, at 2pm. The street runs north to south and eventually leads to Bishopsgate on the north side and down to Aldgate High Street on the south. It is also only a couple of minutes walk from where Eddowes was to die within 12 hours. Catherine told John she was planning to go to Bermondsey to get some money from her daughter. At that time, Ann Conway was actually living at 12 Dilston Grove in Southwark Park Road. She moved frequently to avoid being troubled by her mother. Catherine said she would return by 4pm. John Kelly warned her to beware of the East End murderer, but Catherine replied, 'Don't you fear for me. I shall take care of myself and I shan't fall into his hands'.

Nothing more is known of Catherine until 8.30pm. By that time, a small crowd had gathered outside a building in Aldgate High Street, a few doors east of Aldgate Tube station. Though unnumbered at the time, it is commonly referred to as 29. It was a business premises but appears to have been unoccupied. PC Louis Robinson approached the group to find Catherine Eddowes lying on the ground trying to sleep. From the 1960s onwards, books on the subject sometimes state

Houndsditch, *c.1905.*

Houndsditch, 2007.

Aldgate looking east from Aldgate Pump, *c.1920*.

Aldgate looking east from Aldgate Pump, 2007.

The location of 29 Aldgate High Street, 2004.

that bystanders told him she had just finished a drunken impersonation of a fire engine. He attempted to stand her up but she slipped and fell against the shutters of the building. With the assistance of PC George Simmons she was eventually taken, with some difficulty, to Bishopsgate Police Station (opened in 1865), 10 minutes walk to the north-west. On arrival and being asked her name, she replied 'Nothing'. Sergeant Byfield put her in a cell to sleep off the drink. Twenty minutes later, PC Robinson checked on Eddowes and she was by now asleep. At 9.45pm, PC George Hutt

Black Horse Yard looking towards Aldgate High Street, from *Wonderful London*, 1926.

came on duty at the station and checked on the prisoners in the cells at regular intervals. Eddowes woke at about 11.45pm and half an hour later she was singing softly to herself in the cell. At 12.30am she asked if she could be released. Hutt told her she could be released when she was capable of taking care of herself. She replied she was 'able to do that now'. At 1am, just as Liz Stride's body was being discovered in Dutfield's Yard, Hutt released Catherine Eddowes.

Bishopsgate Police Station, from *Living London*, 1901.

'What time is it?', she asked him.

'Too late for you to get any more drink.'

'Well, what time is it?'

'Just on one.'

'I shall get a damn fine hiding when I get home then', she observed.

'And serves you right – you have no right to get drunk', was Hutt's unsympathetic response.

Bishopsgate Police Station, 2007. The present building was built in 1939 on the same site as the old one and was badly damaged during World War Two.

Bishopsgate, 1895. Liverpool Street Station is on the left. Bishopsgate Police Station is just past the prominent white building on the right.

Bishopsgate, 2007.

Before being discharged, Hutt took down the information Eddowes gave him. Unsurprisingly, she gave an alias and a false address. She said her name was Mary Ann Kelly (very nearly the name of the next Ripper victim, a coincidence that has given fuel to some of the more ridiculous conspiracy theories over the years) and that she lived at 6 Fashion Street. This street still exists, directly north of where Flower and Dean Street used to stand. As Hutt led her to the door he said, 'This way missus', and 'Please pull the door to' when she left. Eddowes's final recorded words were 'All right then. Good night, old cock'. Instead of taking a right turn to head back towards Cooney's, she turned left and probably headed back down Houndsditch towards Aldgate.

It is possible she was heading towards St Botolph's Church at the intersection of several roads including Duke's Place, Houndsditch, Aldgate High Street, Jewry Street, the Minories, and where Fenchurch Street and Leadenhall Street joined together to make Aldgate. There has probably been a church at that location for over a thousand years but the current church was built in the 1740s and designed by George Dance the Elder. The current peal of eight bells is the same as would have been heard in 1888, although they were restored at about that time. The interior was badly damaged by fire in 1965 but was reopened the following year. The church also houses the oldest church organ in London, which is 300 years old.

St Botolph's also has the dubious honour of being known as the Prostitutes' Church, although this name may be more modern than many think. According to legend, in 1888 the Metropolitan Police Force was overburdened with work and decided to come to an arrangement with the plethora of prostitutes in Whitechapel. They granted them an amnesty on condition they confined their soliciting to outside of St Botolph's Church. There was also a demand that they should not stop moving. Because the front of the church was the busiest area, each night a passer-by would

St Botolph's, Aldgate, from the
Minories, c.1905.

see a line of prostitutes all walking in the same direction round and round the church, but speeding up when they had passed the Aldgate High Street side and slowing down when they returned. Though it is well-known that prostitutes did frequently ply for trade outside the church, there is no proof that this tale is otherwise true, not least because St Botolph's is not in the Metropolitan Police area. It has to remain conjectural, but it is possible that this is where Catherine Eddowes was heading.

Shortly before midnight, Albert Bachert entered the Three Nuns Hotel on Aldgate High Street, positioned between St Botolph's Church and Aldgate Tube station. After refusing to buy some matches from an elderly woman, he was approached by a man who commented that such people were a nuisance. Bachert declined the man's offer of a drink, and in his own words:

> He then asked a number of questions about the women of the neighbourhood and their ages etc. He asked if I could tell him where they usually visited. He went outside and spoke to the woman, and gave her something, I believe. He was a dark man, height about 5′6″ or 5′7″. He wore a black felt hat, dark clothes, morning coat, black tie and carried a black shiny bag.

The Three Nuns Tavern, from *The Building News*, 26 April 1878.

At 1.30am, James Blenkingsop (a night watchman overlooking road works in St James's Place, a small square behind and to the west of St Botolph's) claimed to have seen a respectably dressed man who approached him and asked if he had seen a man and woman passing through. Blenkingsop had indeed seen people passing, but had not paid any attention to them.

At the same time, PC Edward Watkins was entering Mitre Square. Mitre Square is a small cobbled area leading off from Mitre Street in the City of London. To its north is a small passage leading into St James's Place and to its east is another passage leading in the direction of St Botolph's. This is now called St James's Passage, but in 1888 it was named Church

The Orange Market, St James's Place, 1850.

Passage. It is now about four metres wide although until the late 20th century it was little more than a metre wide. Mitre Square is built around the cloister of the 12th century Priory of the Holy Trinity. Small fragments of the priory still exist, preserved in a nearby office block on the edge of Mitre Street and Leadenhall Street.

All that exists today of Mitre Square from 1888 is the rough shape and some of the cobbles. Even most of these have been replaced. Beyond this, it has changed entirely beyond recognition. Firstly, it was very dark in the square at night. There were only three dim gas lamps, and these – when working at full capacity – only gave off about the same light as one would get from a modern day refrigerator. One lamp was in Mitre Street, casting very little light into Mitre Square. A second was in the north-east corner and a third was attached to a building at the Mitre Square end of Church Passage. With the exception of the road entering from Mitre Street, the square was surrounded on all four sides, mostly by tall warehouse buildings. Williams & Co. had a warehouse in the north-western corner, Horner and Co. occupied most of the south side and Kearley & Tonge (a trader in tea, spices and confectionery, still functioning well into the middle of the 20th century) ran warehouses along the east and northern sides. There were two houses in Mitre Square. The only family living there was that of PC Richard Pearce. Their house was at 3 Mitre Square, sandwiched between Williams & Co. and an empty house next door. Finally, occupying the south-west corner of the square was the back of an empty house and the back of a picture-

Mitre Square, *c.*1925. This photograph was taken by William Whiffin, one of the most prolific photographers of London's East End.

Church Passage from Mitre Square, September 1961. The door on the left led to George Morris's office. *(Courtesy Margaret Whitby-Green)*

framing shop owned by a Mr Taylor. Both buildings had their fronts on Mitre Street. The only man who would usually be awake in Mitre Square at night was the night watchman of Kearley & Tonge; a retired police officer named George James Morris. His office was in the Kearley & Tonge, building on the east side of Mitre Square.

As PC Watkins entered Mitre Square, his first duty was to look in the south-west corner, as there were two coalholes there at that time for the buildings in Mitre Street and he needed to ensure that no one had removed the covers. Having done this, he would shine his lantern around the other corners of the square before continuing up Mitre Street. His beat would bring him back to Mitre Square about every 15 minutes. At 1.30am he saw nothing unusual.

Five minutes later, three men were walking in the direction of Aldgate High Street having just left the Imperial Club at 16–17 Duke Street. They were Joseph Lawende (a commercial traveller in the cigarette trade), Joseph Hyam Levy (a butcher) and Harry Harris (a furniture dealer). Where Church Passage ran at a right angle from Duke's Place, the group saw a couple talking. This may well have been Catherine Eddowes and her murderer. The woman was wearing a black jacket and bonnet. She was facing the man and had her hand upon his chest. The man was described by

Mitre Square from Mitre Street, September 1961. *(Courtesy Margaret Whitby-Green)*

Lawende as being about 30 years old, 5ft 7 or 8in tall, of medium build and fair complexion with a moustache. He was wearing a loose-fitting pepper and salt coloured jacket and a grey cloth cap with a peak. He also had a red coloured handkerchief round his neck and the general appearance of a sailor. Lawende would later identify Catherine Eddowes's clothes as being the ones he had seen on the woman at the top of Church Passage. Passing the couple with an air of suspicion and distaste, Levy remarked to Harris, 'Look there; I don't like going home by myself when I see those characters about'.

Shortly after this, at 1.40am, PC James Harvey was on his beat along Duke's Place and the vicinity. He walked down the length of the alleyway that made up Church Passage and stopped just before entering Mitre Square, as this was not one of his responsibilities. He did, however, look into the square and, perhaps not surprisingly in the darkness, saw nothing. However, as it was a small and enclosed space, the acoustics in Mitre Square would amplify sound . Harvey also heard nothing and it may well be that Catherine's killer was directly in front of the policeman, motionless and concealed by the night. If this is true, then his luck was little short of miraculous.

Just four minutes later, at 1.44am, Watkins returned on his beat to Mitre Square. Again, he

Mitre Square from St James's Place, September **1961.** *(Courtesy Margaret Whitby-Green)*

Mitre Square from St James's Place, 2007.

Duke's Place Synagogue, *c.*1905. Church Passage is at the lower left of the photo.

immediately turned right to inspect the corner, but this time his lantern picked up more than rain-soaked flagstones. He immediately ran over to the door of Kearley & Tonge, which was slightly ajar, and summoned George Morris with 'For God's sake, mate, come to my assistance'. Morris replied, 'Stop until I get my lamp. What is the matter?' Watkins responded with a dramatic but nevertheless accurate 'There's another woman been ripped to pieces'. Morris asked where the body was and Watkins answered that she was in the corner.

Morris crossed to the corner and turned his lamp on the form just perceptible on the pavement. When he'd seen the carnage for himself, he ran up Mitre Street and into Aldgate, blowing his whistle to summon help, while PC Watkins remained with the body. Morris met PCs Harvey and Holland, who asked him what the matter was. He told them about the body in Mitre Square and they followed him to the spot, after which Morris returned to his position in Kearley & Tonge.

The first medical official to arrive was Dr George William Sequeira, who lived at 34 Jewry Street, no more than two minutes walk to the south of Mitre Square. He arrived just 10 minutes

Ripper's Corner, from *Jack the Ripper, A New Theory* by William Stewart, 1938.

Ripper's Corner, 2007.

The Kearley & Tonge warehouses, with ghosts of the lettering still visible, September 1961. *(Courtesy Margaret Whitby-Green)*

after the discovery of the body and gave a cursory inspection. The London Police Surgeon, Dr Frederick Gordon Brown, was also sent for and arrived shortly after 2am. He described the position of the body and mutilations thus:

> The body was on its back, the head turned to left shoulder. The arms by the side of the body as if they had fallen there. Both palms upwards, the fingers slightly bent. The left leg extended in a line with the body. The abdomen was exposed. Right leg bent at the thigh and knee. The throat cut across.
>
> The intestines were drawn out to a large extent and placed over the right shoulder - they were smeared over with some feculent matter. A piece of about two feet was quite detached from the body and placed between the body and the left arm, apparently by design. The lobe and auricle of the right ear were cut obliquely through.
>
> There was a quantity of clotted blood on the pavement on the left side of the neck round the shoulder and upper part of arm, and fluid blood-coloured serum which had flowed under the neck to the right shoulder, the pavement sloping in that direction.
>
> Body was quite warm. No death stiffening had taken place. She must have been dead most likely within the half hour. We looked for superficial bruises and saw none. No blood on the skin of the abdomen or secretion of any kind on the thighs. No spurting of blood on the bricks or pavement

The site of 34 Jewry Street, 2007.

around. No marks of blood below the middle of the body. Several buttons were found in the clotted blood after the body was removed. There was no blood on the front of the clothes. There were no traces of recent connexion.

As the discovery had been made within the City of London, the body was taken north to the mortuary at Golden Lane, just south of Old Street and in the general area of the Barbican. By the time Catherine's remains had arrived, a quantity of blood had soaked into the clothing through the jostling of the body on a covered handcart being pushed through the streets. Her face had also been terribly and deliberately disfigured after death. It had been slashed diagonally several times down to the right, cutting the upper gum. The tip of her nose had been hacked off, the eyelids cut through vertically and inverted Vs had been nicked into each cheek. As her clothing was removed, her right ear lobe – which had been cut off by one of the diagonal strokes – fell from her clothing. Her left kidney and uterus had been removed and were missing.

Golden Lane Coroners Court, *c.*1941.

Shortly after Dr Brown had been sent for, Bishopsgate Police Station Inspector Edward Collard was informed of the murder at 1.55am. He arrived at Mitre Square about the same time as Brown. While Collard was being told about the scene in Mitre Square, detective constables Halse, Marriott and Outram (who were all nearby) heard the news and immediately set out in different directions to search for the culprit.

Major Henry Smith was the Acting Commissioner of the City of London Police and on the night of the Eddowes murder was attempting to sleep above Cloak Lane Police Station. He was eventually summoned and was taken in a cab to Mitre Square. In his memoirs, Smith recalls the events in a far more melodramatic style with more than a hint of bravado, but he was known to be a raconteur with little to substantiate his tales.

Golden Lane, 2006. The Coroners Court was situated just before the building on the left.

Goulston Street runs north to south, parallel with Commercial Street in the east and Middlesex Street (also known as Petticoat Lane) in the west, just within the boundary of Whitechapel. At its northern end it terminates at the junction with Wentworth Street – one of the most deprived thoroughfares in the area at that time and beloved of the artist Gustav Doré – and continues north as Bell Lane. Still standing at the top end on the eastern side are Wentworth Model Dwellings, built in 1887. In the late 1970s the street had become almost derelict and there were plans to knock the building down. Wentworth Model Dwellings formed a long tenement block with several doorways leading up sets of stairs to individual rooms, like many other residential blocks of the period. It opened out onto the busy cloth market of Goulston Street and the majority of the residents were Jewish. The second staircase down from the Wentworth Street junction was the entrance to rooms 108–119. About four feet in through the doorway, a set of stairs on the right led up to the first floor while, on the left, stairs led down to the basement (some of the basement steps still exist, out of public view). These stairs remained until 1990 when, after years of being bricked up, they were removed by the current owner, who incorporated the space into

Cloak Lane Police Station, 2006. The building ceased to be used as a police station in 1965.

the Happy Days fish and chips takeaway and restaurant, directly to the right and still trading in 2007. Above the doorway on the left was attached a small metal sign bearing the numbers of the rooms above.

At 2.20am, PC Alfred Long 254A – who had been drafted in from Westminster to bolster the number of police on the streets in Whitechapel during the Ripper scare – walked past Wentworth Model Dwellings and saw nothing unusual. When he next passed, at 2.55am, he shone his lantern into the open doorway leading to the staircase for rooms 108–119 and discovered, just behind the door jamb on the right of the doorway, half a white apron – a considerable amount of cloth, as Victorian aprons mostly ran up

The site of the City Police Headquarters, 26 Old Jewry, 2007.

Goulston Street from Wentworth Street, *c.*1907. Wentworth Model Dwellings are on the left.

to the chest rather than the waist – which was smothered in blood and faeces. A corner of the apron was also wet with blood. It is to be assumed that the killer had cut this piece of apron from Catherine's clothing (and it was indeed hers, as it was found to be a perfect match to the piece remaining on her body) and had used it to wipe his hands and knife clean when retreating from the scene of the crime. It may also have been used to transport her internal organs, which were never recovered.

Just above the apron, on the jamb of the open doorway, was a curious phrase written in white chalk. It read 'The Juwes are The men That Will not be blamed for nothing' according to the notes made by PC Long, or 'The Juwes are not The men That Will be blamed for nothing' as later transcribed by Halse from the City Police. Much has been made in more recent years of the misspelling of the word 'Juwes' (clearly meaning 'Jews'). It was suggested in the early 1970s that the term 'Juwes' was a Masonic reference, relating to the murder of Grand Master Hiram Abiff by three artisan stonemasons named Jubela, Jubelo and Jubelum. However, this ritual had been dropped from Masonic ceremony in England some years before and collectively the three killers are known as the Ruffians. 'Juwes' has no known meaning in any language. Ripper historians are split over the significance of this writing today, but the majority feel it has no connection to the

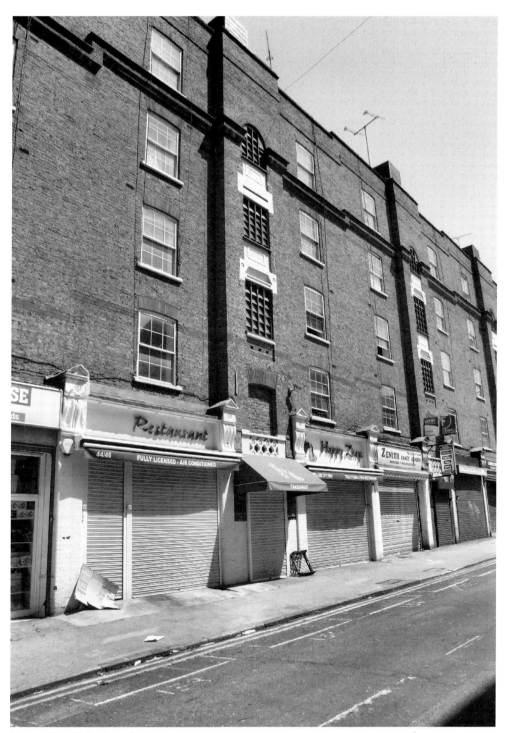

Wentworth Model Dwellings, Goulston Street, 2007.

killer and was probably nothing more than a confused anti-Semitic protest. There were even witnesses who felt the writing was smudged, as if it had been there for some time.

It was not long before there were several officers from both the City Police (from the area of the murder) and the Metropolitan Police (as the apron was found in their jurisdiction) in Goulston Street. Superintendent Thomas Arnold of H Division wanted to keep the peace in the district and, aware of the inflammatory nature of the writing on the wall at Wentworth Model Dwellings, sent an Inspector with a wet sponge to Goulston Street to remove the writing before it could be seen by the public who would, within a few hours, be milling about outside. This act is often considered to be one of the most foolhardy in the whole police investigation, as it was, at face value, the destruction of evidence. However, this has to be evaluated against the anti-Semitic feeling in parts of London at that time and the opinions on the provenance of the message. It has been suggested that perhaps the writing could have been covered up and then quickly photographed to record it for posterity, but in actuality this would have been very difficult to achieve, at the entrance of a residential building opening onto a busy

Entrance to 108–119 Wentworth Model Dwellings, 1975. *(Courtesy Richard Whittington-Egan)*

The same entrance, 2007.

marketplace. The one criticism we can perhaps have today is concerning the discrepancy of the wording and the notion that perhaps the style of handwriting should have been accurately recreated as well. Records describe the graffito as being in 'perfectly rounded schoolboy hand' and nothing more.

It also needs to be considered that this doorway would have been very dark indeed, as the only dim gas lamp in that part of Goulston Street was about 20 yards north, although there was another lamp on the corner by New Goulston Street. It would not have been easy, on that particular night, for a killer fleeing from both the City and Metropolitan Police Forces to dispose of a piece of damning evidence and then linger to write a nonsensical message with chalk he had contrived to have about his person.

The Inspector with the wet sponge took no action, and awaited the arrival of no less a person than Sir Charles Warren, head of the Metropolitan Police. Upon inspecting the writing at 5.30am, as the sun was rising in the sky, Warren agreed with Arnold's opinion and the writing was duly erased, a simple act which still causes disagreements between students of the case to this day.

Catherine Eddowes's body was identified separately by both her paramour John Kelly and her sister Eliza Gold on 2 October. John Kelly had only become aware of the murder after reading in a newspaper that one of the victims on the night of the Double Event (as it has passed into Ripper lore) had in her possession a pawn ticket in the name of Birrell and a tattoo 'TC' on her forearm. He had already been informed that Catherine had been locked up at Bishopsgate on the Saturday night for drunkenness.

Catherine's funeral was held on 8 October 1888. She, like Polly Nichols, was buried in a common grave in the City of London Cemetery. The two bodies rest only a few yards apart. Also like Polly, in recent years she has been given a small monument close to the burial plot.

Although Mitre Square still exudes the same atmosphere as it did in 1888, due to its small size, the cobbles on the roadway and the comparative peace and quiet next to so many busy roads, none of the buildings from the time of the Ripper remain. All the structures were replaced or removed piece by piece from the 1940s until the 1980s. Nobody lives in Mitre Square today. On the south side is the playground for the Sir John Cass Foundation School. Where Williams & Co. traded there is a high wall, on top of which rests a shrubbery. Church Passage is now St James's Passage and is four times as wide, with a café on one side. Where George Morris had his office there is a barrier and a small car parking area beyond it. A large, unoccupied office block stands where the main Kearley & Tonge building once loomed over the murder scene. Brown shutters to an inside car park mark the house of PC Pearce. As for the corner where Catherine Eddowes died, that still retains a curious ambience. There are no buildings on that spot today. A large flowerbed with benches on two sides marks the site of Mr Taylor's shop on Mitre Street and part of the empty house next door. The furthest part of the corner now has a path running through it to Mitre Street and the Aldgate Pump beyond. The spot where Eddowes died, still sometimes referred to as Ripper's Corner, has also been entirely redeveloped. Under the covering arms of a large tree, the spot today is right on the edge of the kerbstones, about two feet from the wall of the school playground.

On 1 October, another taunting communication turned up at the Central News Agency in New Bridge Street. This is usually referred to as Saucy Jacky Postcard. When news of its arrival was published in *The Star*, the newspaper was already of the belief that the Dear Boss letter was a practical joke. The latest communication appeared to be smeared with blood and read:

> I wa'snt codding dear old Boss when I gave you the tip. You'll hear about saucy Jackys work tomorrow
>
> double event this time number one squealed a bit. Couldn't finish straight off. had not time to get ears
>
> for police. thanks for keeping last letter back till I got to work again. Jack the Ripper

Exactly one week later, bloodhounds were tested successfully in Regents' Park, in a trial beginning at 7am. The two dogs, Barnaby and Burgho, were considered perfect specimens and were to be used in the event of future crimes to sniff the scent of the killer and lead the police to his apprehension. However, such optimism was short-lived, for the following day, Tuesday 9 October, a repeat test was held in Hyde Park, this time with Sir Charles Warren as bait. The dogs disappeared in the fog and lost track of the scent. This well-intentioned failure meant that Warren, already the subject of dissatisfaction, lost a good deal of public face. Following the second trial, the Metropolitan Police declined to buy the dogs.

On the evening of 16 October, the Chairman of the Whitechapel Vigilance Committee, George Lusk, received a letter and small parcel at his home in Mile End. Although it is highly unlikely that any of the many letters claiming to be from the killer are genuine, this one possibly comes closest to being authentic:

> Mr Lusk
>
> Sor
>
> I send you half the Kidne I took from one women prasarved it for you tother piece I fried and ate it
>
> was very nise I may send you the bloody knif that took it out if you only wate a whil longer.
>
> Signed Catch me when you can Mishter Lusk

With this letter was enclosed half a human kidney, but at the time he received it, Lusk had no way of knowing that. He mentioned it at a meeting of the Committee the following day at the Crown pub.

The following day, Lusk, Joseph Aarons (the treasurer), B. Harris (the secretary) and two other committee members took the kidney to Dr Frederick Wiles of 56 Mile End Road. He was not at the address at the time, but his assistant, F. S. Reed, gave his opinion that it was human in origin and had been preserved in spirits of wine, not formalin as one would usually have expected. Dr Wiles wanted a second opinion so, in the company of members of the Committee, he took the kidney to Dr Thomas Horrocks Openshaw, Curator of the Pathological Museum at the London Hospital. Openshaw confirmed it was indeed half of a left kidney, and that it was human.

Some myths and suppositions have circulated about the Lusk kidney. Firstly, some have claimed that because the kidney showed signs of Bright's Disease, and Catherine Eddowes was known to have been a sufferer this was proof it came from her. In fact, Bright's Disease was not a rare condition at all in the East End at that time. Some have also said that the kidney came from a middle-aged woman. This would be impossible to tell, and although women's kidneys are

George Lusk's house during the Whitechapel Murders, 1 Tollet Street, Alderney Road, 2007.

usually slightly smaller than men's this is by no means a hard and fast rule. Most importantly of all, it is frequently stated that an inch of renal artery was attached to the Lusk kidney. Two inches of renal artery were left inside the body and the renal artery is three inches long, thus presenting fairly persuasive circumstantial evidence. However, it is simply not true that an inch of renal artery was attached to the kidney. It had actually been cleanly trimmed. There is thus no concrete evidence to suggest this was anything more than an unpleasant but well-executed practical joke.

Some drawings and plans connected to the Eddowes murder were discovered in the basement of the London Hospital in the 1960s and these now form part of a small display on forensic pathology at the hospital's museum.

MARY JANE KELLY

Mary Jane Kelly as found inside 13 Miller's Court. *(Courtesy Donald Rumbelow / Stewart P. Evans)*

There has been a great deal of romance and supposition associated with the youngest Ripper victim, as so little is known about her background. It is even possible that the name the world remembers her by was not her real name but a pseudonym. Most of what has been recorded about her past is nothing more than information she gave to friends in the last couple of years of her life. Occasionally, research brings forth the possibility that fragments of her tales may be true, but it is highly unlikely that her authentic story will ever become public knowledge. Due to the ferocity of the mutilations inflicted upon her body after death, we cannot even say with certainty what she looked like.

Mary's date of birth was estimated as being in 1863, as most sources concur that she died at the age of 25 years. She claimed she had been born in Limerick, Southern Ireland, with six or seven brothers and one sister. One brother, named Henry (though commonly known as John or Johnto), was serving in the 2nd Battalion Scots Guards.

In early childhood, Mary supposedly moved to Wales. Her father, John Kelly, had worked as a foreman at an iron works in either Caernarvonshire or Carmarthenshire. While in Wales, she had

St George Street, 1895.

Breezer's Hill from St George Street
(now called The Highway, 2007.

married a collier named Davies at the age of 16. Her husband had then died in a pit explosion some two or three years afterwards. She then claimed to have moved to Cardiff in about 1883 and stayed in an infirmary there for nine months.

The following year, Mary moved to London and worked as a prostitute in an expensive West End brothel. From connections she had made she left for France at least once but returned to London, as she had not enjoyed the experience. It was after her return that she moved to the East End.

Mary's first known address in the area – if her stories were true – was somewhere off the

St George Street, where she stayed with a Mrs Buki. She then moved from this tenancy to live with a man named Morganstone close to Stepney Gasworks. From here, the picture becomes a little clearer. In 1886 she was living with a Mrs Carthy in Breezer's Hill, again just off St George Street. She left Breezer's Hill to stay with a man called Joseph Fleming, a plasterer or mason living near Bethnal Green Road.

After splitting from Fleming, Mary went to live in Cooly's Lodging House in Thrawl Street. It was while living there that she met, on Good Friday 8 April 1887, a Billingsgate Market fish porter named Joseph Barnett. They were to live together until just before Mary's death. With little income and regularly finding themselves in debt, the couple would frequently move when the bills could not be paid. They stayed variously at George Street, Little Paternoster Row and Brick Lane before moving, in the spring of 1888, to 13 Miller's Court, Dorset Street.

Dorset Street was undoubtedly one of the very worst streets in the whole of London. It was said that even policemen were loath to walk down the street alone. This was an area where the utmost deprivation and depravity could be found. The poorest doss houses, the prostitutes, the violent

Commercial Street from Spitalfields Market, 1907.

drunks, the thieves and knife-wielders all had their place along this road. It lay east to west between Commercial Street in the east and Crispin Street in the west, with the Providence Row Night Refuge and Convent (built 1860 and still standing today, now as a home to a section of the London School of Economics). It was about 130 yards long and fronted with houses largely built in around 1700. Three pubs were to be found here – the Britannia at the junction

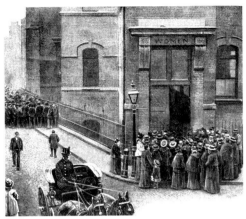

Providence Row, from *Living London*, 1901.

with Commercial Street, the Horn of Plenty at the Crispin Street end, and the Blue Coat Boy roughly halfway between the two. To the north lay Brushfield Street, and directly to the south was White's Row. Across the road on Commercial Street were Christ Church, Spitalfields and the notorious Itchy Park. Itchy Park gained its name because this graveyard was the resting-place of

Providence Row, 2007.

Christ Church, Spitalfields, from Brushfield Street, 1963.

Itchy Park, Christ Church, Spitalfields, *c.*1905.

not only the dead, but also of homeless transients. Those who could not afford lodging or find a bed at the workhouse had to walk the streets at night, as the police would move them on if they found them asleep in doorways. When the gates to Itchy Park were opened in the mornings, these nocturnal nomads would pour in, often paying little heed to the weather conditions, and sleep on the benches, against the monuments and trees, or simply on the grass.

Miller's Court was reached on the north side of Dorset Street, about one quarter of the way along from the east. It was entered via a brick archway, no more than three feet wide and running down about 20 feet into a courtyard. Above the entrance to the alleyway was an iron nameplate bearing the courtyard's name. No photographs exist of the interior of Miller's Court beyond a single image of the exterior of 13, but its layout is well documented. On emerging into the open air at the other end you would have been confronted with a claustrophobic cul-de-sac of dirty cottages, 30 to 40 years old, to your left and right, with a wall and toilets at the end. Immediately to your right, just past 13, there was a small area containing a water pump and refuse facilities. People lived in individual rooms along both sides, one up, one down. Not all the rooms were occupied. 13 Miller's Court differed from the other residences because it was actually part of 26 Dorset Street.

Mary's landlord was a man named John McCarthy, a shopkeeper who owned several low-grade properties that were commonly referred to as 'McCarthy's rents'. McCarthy ran a chandler's shop, selling candles, oils and groceries to the local populace at 27 Dorset Street, on the left-hand side of the Miller's Court archway. 26 was unoccupied at the front, but McCarthy used to store goods there and occasionally allow market traders to store their handcarts inside. People lived on the upper floors of 26, also tenants of McCarthy. One staircase just before the end of the Miller's Court archway and right next to the door of 13 led to the rooms above 26 Dorset Street.

13 Miller's Court was far from palatial. It was a single room, 10 x 12ft in size and partitioned off from the back of 26 Dorset Street. The single door was hinged on the right and the contents of the room hardly extended beyond a bed, two small tables, a wash stand and a fireplace. The bed was behind the door, along the length of the partition wall. A small table lay between the bed and the door. The second table and wash stand were at the end of the bed and set into the opposite wall from the door was the fireplace. The room also had two windows, mismatched and at different levels, set into the wall that looked out into Miller's Court. The difference in these windows has led some to conclude that maybe 13 Miller's Court had at some time been two tiny rooms, such as a lobby and pantry. One of the windows, that closest to the door, had two panes of broken glass which had been stuffed with newspaper

The entrance to Millers Court, June 1928, from *The Mystery of Jack the Ripper* by Leonard Matters.

The same view in 2007. The Spitalfields Fruit Exchange, which occupies the site, is set back about 26 feet from the position of the house fronts in Dorset Street.

Duval Street from Commercial Street, September 1961. *(Courtesy Margaret Whitby-Green)*

and rags to keep out the elements. Either Mary or Joe had caused the breakage during a drunken argument. Mary was known to have a fierce temper when drunk, something that had become more common as time had gone on, though she was placid, quiet and friendly when sober.

Joseph Fleming used to visit Mary while she was living with Joe Barnett in Miller's Court. In July 1888, Barnett lost his job. On 30 October 1888 the couple had their final row. Mary was allowing a prostitute friend called Maria Harvey to sleep on the floor of the small room and Joe,

Duval Street from Crispin Street, September 1961.
(Courtesy Margaret Whitby-Green)

Duval Street from Crispin Street, 2007.

naturally, objected to this arrangement. He then moved to Buller's Lodging House at 24–25 New Street, Bishopsgate. New Street remains, very close to Liverpool Street station, but Buller's has long since disappeared. The location is right next to the modern Bishopsgate Police Station. In spite of their separation, Mary and Joe remained on good terms and he would visit her at Miller's Court on an almost daily basis.

On Thursday 8 November, Joe made one of these stops between 7 and 8pm. When he arrived, Mary was in the company of another woman who lived in Miller's Court. This might have been a woman named Lizzie Albrook,

13 Millers Court, 8 November 1888. *(Courtesy Donald Rumbelow / Stewart P. Evans)*

who was on good terms with Mary. Lizzie claimed that Mary had once mentioned having a cousin who worked on the stage. Maria Harvey was also later to state that she had been in Mary Kelly's room and had left shortly before 7pm. Mary's female guest and Joe Barnett both departed at about 8pm and Joe returned to Buller's in New Street.

New Street, Bishopsgate, 2007. Buller's Lodging House was situated approximately where the crates can be seen on the left.

The Ten Bells public house, *c.1905*. A notorious haunt for prostitutes, it was said Mary Kelly plied her trade here.

Maurice Lewis, a tailor living in Dorset Street, claimed to have seen Mary Kelly between 10pm and 11pm in the Horn of Plenty pub. She was drinking with some other women and with Joe Barnett. In press reports, Lewis calls the man Dan, so it may have been Joe's brother, Daniel. Lewis also said that one of the women he had seen with Mary was known to him as Julia. This would almost certainly have been Julia Venturney, a widowed charwoman who lived at 1 Miller's Court.

At 11.45pm, Mary Ann Cox, a 31-year-old widow and prostitute who lived at the far left-hand end of Miller's Court, came into Dorset Street from Commercial Street. As it was cold and raining, she had decided to return home to get warm. She saw Mary Kelly and a man of large build walking ahead of her. The man was in his mid-30s and about 5ft 5in tall. He was shabbily dressed in dark clothes and a long, dark overcoat with a billycock hat. He had a blotchy face, small side-whiskers and a carroty moustache. Mary Ann Cox also noticed he was carrying a quart pot of beer. Both Mary Kelly and the man appeared to be very drunk.

Mary Ann Cox followed Mary Kelly and her companion down the passage into Miller's Court and greeted Mary as she passed at the door to 13. Mary mumbled in return that she was going to sing for the man she had brought back. A few minutes later, Cox was to hear Mary Kelly at the other end of the courtyard singing the popular mawkish Victorian music hall ballad *Only A Violet I Plucked From Mother's Grave*. When Cox returned to Commercial Street at midnight, Mary was still singing the same song. It would also have been around this time that Mary Kelly had her final meal of fish and potatoes – this could well have been fish and chips.

Dorset Street looking east, from *Living London*, 1901.

Houses in Millers Court, from *The Weekly Dispatch*, 11 November 1888.

The Horn of Plenty from Crispin Street, 20 April 1912.

By half past midnight, Mary Kelly's singing had begun to annoy her neighbours. One of them, a flower seller named Catherine Pickett, was about to knock on her door to complain, but was stopped from going downstairs by her husband.

At 1am, Mary Ann Cox returned to 5 Miller's Court to warm herself again. Mary Kelly was still singing and light was coming from behind the windows. After a few minutes in her room, Cox left again.

Directly above 13 Miller's Court was room 20 of 26 Dorset Street, reached from the staircase near to the entrance to Mary Kelly's door. It is possible that the numbering continued from 14 and above inside 26 Dorset Street. The woman who lived above Mary Kelly was called Elizabeth Prater, the estranged wife of William Prater, a boot finisher who had left her five years previously. There were only floorboards keeping the two rooms apart, and almost every sound from the room below could be heard upstairs. Even chinks of light came through the gaps in the boards. At about 1.30am, Prater went up to her room after having spent half an hour at the entrance to Miller's Court waiting for a man. Nothing could be heard from Mary's room, although some light was visible. Prater placed two chairs against the door as a means of security and went to bed without getting undressed.

At 2am, George Hutchinson had just reached Commercial Street, having walked back from Romford, some miles further to the east. He was a resident at the Victoria Working Men's Home further down Commercial Street, on the south-western junction of Wentworth Street. On reaching Thrawl Street (the next street up on the right) he passed a man but paid no attention to him. At Flower and Dean Street he met Mary Kelly, who was known to him. She asked Hutchinson to loan her sixpence, but he was unable to do so, having spent all the money he had making the journey to Romford. She started to walk in the direction from which Hutchinson had just come, leaving him with 'Good morning, I must go and find some money'. By this time, the man Hutchinson had passed at Thrawl Street was walking towards them and as Hutchinson walked

The Victoria Home, Commercial Street, from *The People of the Abyss* by Jack London, 1902.

away, the stranger approached Mary Kelly. He put his hand on her shoulder and she laughed. Hutchinson then heard Mary say 'All right' and the man reply with 'You will be all right for what I have told you'. The man placed his right hand on Mary's shoulder and they began to walk up Commercial Street in the direction of Dorset Street.

Hutchinson had by this time reached the Queen's Head pub (still standing but unused) on the junction with Fashion Street, directly above Flower and Dean Street and on the opposite side of the street to the eastern end of White's Row. He stood under a lamppost as the couple approached him. This is when he got a good look

The site of the Victoria Home, 2007.

at the man with Mary Kelly, who returned his gaze with a stern glare. The description is so detailed it has caused some to question its authenticity:

> Age about 34 or 35. Height 5′6″. Complexion pale, dark eyes and eye lashes, slight moustache, curled up each end, and hair dark. Very surly looking. Dress: long dark coat, collar and cuffs trimmed astrakhan and a dark jacket under, light waistcoat, dark trousers, dark felt hat turned down in the middle, button boots and gaiters with white buttons. Wore a very thick gold chain. White linen collar, black tie with horse shoe pin. Respectable appearance. Walked very sharp. Jewish appearance. Can be identified.

Hutchinson did not come forward or make a statement until some days later, just after the inquest into Mary's death had been held. In spite of the extensive list of ostensibly costly garments, Hutchinson also observed that the man with Kelly was 'shabby genteel', which implied the clothing was past its best. In a further statement, Hutchinson was to embellish the sighting by adding that the man had bushy eyebrows, a large seal on the gold chain with a red stone hanging from it and was carrying kid gloves in his right hand and a small package in the left.

Mary Kelly and the man crossed Commercial Street and turned down Dorset Street. Hutchinson followed them at a distance. The couple stopped at the Miller's Court entrance and Hutchinson heard Kelly tell the man 'All right, my dear, come along. You will be comfortable'.

Commercial Street from Thrawl Street, September 1961. *(Courtesy Margaret Whitby-Green)*

The Queen's Head public house, 2007.

The man then put his arm around Kelly and she kissed him and commented that she had lost her handkerchief. At this he handed her a red handkerchief and they walked down towards her room. Hutchinson remained at the same spot for nearly an hour, standing by a lamp next to the Crossingham's lodging house opposite the archway. By the time the bells of Christ Church rang at 3am just yards away, Hutchinson decided that he was wasting his time. It was cold and wet and he was locked out of the Victoria Home for the night, so he left to find somewhere to sleep.

It was at about the same moment that Mary Ann Cox returned to her room for a third time, this time for the rest of the night. Now there was no sound or light from 13 Miller's Court. She remained awake for the rest of the night and several times heard men going in and out of the court. She heard someone

Crossingham's Lodging House, 17 Dorset Street (later Duval Street), September 1961. *(Courtesy Margaret Whitby-Green)*

leaving one of the rooms at about 5.45am, but she did not hear a door shut afterwards and was unable to ascertain which address it had been.

At 4am Elizabeth Prater, asleep in Room 20 above, was woken by her pet kitten, Diddles, walking over her neck. From nearby she heard a faint cry of 'Oh, murder!' Sarah Lewis, staying at 2 Miller's Court, also heard the cry. It is difficult to say, from this distance, if this cry was connected to the murder of Mary Kelly in any way. It was a fairly common shout, especially in an area like Dorset Street, and it seems unlikely that a victim of crime would shout such a thing when 'Help!' would have been quicker and more direct.

At 8.30am on 9 November (the day of the Lord Mayor's Parade), Caroline Maxwell, the wife of a lodging-house keeper, claimed she saw Mary Kelly in Dorset Street just outside Miller's Court. It appears she did not know Mary as well as she suggested and her testimony was not taken too seriously as it was in direct conflict with most of the other reports. Maxwell asked Mary why she was up so early and Mary had replied that she was suffering from the effects of alcohol, and had been for some days. Maxwell suggested that perhaps it would be an idea to take a drink at the

Britannia to ward off the effects of withdrawal, but Mary had replied that, already having done so, she had vomited and indicated where she had thrown up on the road. Maxwell then claimed to have seen Mary again at 9am outside the Britannia, talking to a man who resembled a market porter.

Just after 10am, Maurice Lewis had been playing a ball game with others in Miller's Court and on hearing a boy yell the warning 'Copper!' he and his companions had quickly left and gone into the Britannia. He was positive that when he entered the pub, he had seen Mary Kelly drinking with some other people, but could not say if any men were in the group. He eventually left again and returned to his house at about 10.30am and 30 minutes later was informed that Mary Kelly had been found dead in her room.

At 10.45am, John McCarthy was in his shop at 27 Dorset Street and sent an employee, Thomas Bowyer, to collect monies owed by Mary Kelly. At this point she was in arrears to the sum of 29 shillings, which would have been a huge amount to someone in her position. Rent had not been paid for six weeks. Upon reaching the door of 13 Miller's Court, Bowyer knocked twice but was unable to gain an answer. Knowing two window panes were broken and had been sealed in a very temporary manner, he went around the corner of the building and pulled out the paper and textiles in one of the frames. Having done this, he put his hand through the hole and took hold of the curtain, sheet, coat, or whatever else has been suggested was covering the inside of the window. Pulling it aside, he presumed that Mary Kelly was in her room, quietly ignoring his calls for her to pay the money she owed.

The room was in semi-darkness as little sunlight reached into Miller's Court and the day was decidedly inclement. It took Bowyer a little time for his eyes to adjust, but eventually he saw what appeared to be a mound of flesh on the small table at the head of the bed. On looking a second time, he noticed the walls were covered in blood and there was a body on the bed. Reeling from the window, he staggered up Miller's Court and told McCarthy what he had seen. Both men returned to the window and McCarthy saw the body for himself. As soon as he had done so, both men ran out of Miller's Court, turned left along Dorset Street and then left again a few hundred yards up Commercial Street towards the Commercial Street Police Station, occupying a triangular island by Fleur De Lis Street and Elder Street. The same building, built in 1876 still stands today, albeit decommissioned, and with the addition of an extra floor built in 1906. Some members of the police force know it by the name Comical Street, because of its unusual shape.

McCarthy and Bowyer spoke to Inspector Walter Beck and he and Detective Constable Walter

Commercial Street Police Station, 2007.

Dew (the man who arrested Dr Crippen in 1910) returned to Miller's Court with the men. When Beck saw the carnage through the window for himself, he said, 'For God's sake, Dew, don't look!' The tableau Dew saw for himself was to stay with him for the rest of his life. John McCarthy was later to comment:

> It looked more like the work of the devil than of a man. I had heard a great deal about the Whitechapel murders, but I declare to God I had never expected to see such a sight as this. The whole scene is more than I can describe. I hope I may never see such a sight as this again.

The men quickly decided not to enter the room because it was a crime scene and would, perhaps, be of use to the bloodhounds Barnaby and Burgho if they could be brought to the site. The police awaited instruction from higher places. And they continued to wait. The bloodhounds did not arrive, and Sir Charles Warren had resigned his post the previous day. It was not until approximately 1.30pm, nearly three hours after the discovery of the body, that access was gained. It is said that John McCarthy himself prised open the door with a pickaxe under the orders of Superintendent Arnold (though some accounts erroneously state he broke it down with a sledgehammer).

When the police entered the room they found Mary Kelly's clothes neatly folded on a chair and her boots in front of the fireplace. A fierce fire had been burning, so intense that it had melted the spout of a kettle. Among the ashes were several burnt items of clothing, which had acted as fuel. These were found to belong to Maria Harvey.

Dr Thomas Bond was to describe the condition of the remains of Mary Kelly as follows:

The body was lying naked in the middle of the bed, the shoulders flat but the axis of the body inclined to the left side of the bed. The head was turned on the left cheek. The left arm was close to the body with the forearm flexed at a right angle and lying across the abdomen.

The right arm was slightly abducted from the body and rested on the mattress. The elbow was bent, the forearm supine with the fingers clenched. The legs were wide apart, the left thigh at right angles to the trunk and the right forming an obtuse angle with the pubes.

The whole of the surface of the abdomen and thighs was removed and the abdominal cavity emptied of its viscera. The breasts were cut off, the arms mutilated by several jagged wounds and the face hacked beyond recognition of the features. The tissues of the neck were severed all round down to the bone.

The viscera were found in various parts viz: the uterus and kidneys with one breast under the head, the other breast by the right foot, the liver between the feet, the intestines by the right side and the spleen by the left side of the body. The flaps removed from the abdomen and thighs were on a table.

The bed clothing at the right corner was saturated with blood, and on the floor beneath was a pool of blood covering about two feet square. The wall by the right side of the bed and in a line with the neck was marked by blood which had struck it in a number of separate splashes.

The face was gashed in all directions, the nose, cheeks, eyebrows, and ears being partly removed. The lips were blanched and cut by several incisions running obliquely down to the chin. There were also numerous cuts extending irregularly across all the features.

The neck was cut through the skin and other tissues right down to the vertebrae, the fifth and sixth being deeply notched. The skin cuts in the front of the neck showed distinct ecchymosis. The air passage was cut at the lower part of the larynx through the cricoid cartilage.

Both breasts were more or less removed by circular incisions, the muscle down to the ribs being attached to the breasts. The intercostals between the fourth, fifth, and sixth ribs were cut through and the contents of the thorax visible through the openings.

The skin and tissues of the abdomen from the costal arch to the pubes were removed in three large flaps. The right thigh was denuded in front to the bone, the flap of skin, including the external organs of generation, and part of the right buttock. The left thigh was stripped of skin fascia, and muscles as far as the knee.

The left calf showed a long gash through skin and tissues to the deep muscles and reaching from the knee to five inches above the ankle. Both arms and forearms had extensive jagged wounds.

The right thumb showed a small superficial incision about one inch long, with extravasation of blood in the skin, and there were several abrasions on the back of the hand moreover showing the same condition.

On opening the thorax it was found that the right lung was minimally adherent by old firm adhesions. The lower part of the lung was broken and torn away. The left lung was intact. It was adherent at the apex and there were a few adhesions over the side. In the substances of the lung there were several nodules of consolidation.

The pericardium was open below and the heart absent. In the abdominal cavity there was some partly digested food of fish and potatoes, and similar food was found in the remains of the stomach attached to the intestines.

Upon inspection of the infamous photograph of Mary Kelly, it seems that this account is remarkably accurate. However, a debate still continues to this day about the possibility that she was naked. Many researchers feel she was wearing a chemise, a view strengthened by the testimony of Dr Phillips, who stated this, and the puff of material seen on her left arm could either be a garment or part of the bedding. Also, on the image (taken by the photographer Joseph Martin) it appears that at least some of her intestines were placed over her genitalia. Mary's face was so mutilated that it is not even possible to establish where her features were, and several students of the case have very different opinions. All that can clearly be seen in the image is her hairline.

The body was eventually collected in a hand-carted ambulance and a battered coffin shell was brought out for the journey to Shoreditch Mortuary. The arrival of the undertaker caused a rush of people, who could barely be contained.

Shoreditch Mortuary lay behind St Leonard's Church in Shoreditch High Street, half a mile directly north of Dorset Street. The church has ancient origins and Will Somers, jester to Henry VIII, and the Shakespearean actor Richard Burbage, are both buried within. The current building was completed in 1740 and looked very much as it does today. In the crypt are numerous opened vaults containing dozens of early 19th-century coffins, many containing victims of scarlet fever or cholera. During the 1950s, this crypt was actually used as a meeting place for the local Scout

Troop. Today, St Leonard's is often locked and groups of homeless alcoholics congregate on its steps. The mortuary, at the eastern end of the church in a separate single-storey building like that at St George's in the East, was a simple affair and has long since disappeared. A dilapidated storage shed stands on the spot today.

It took six hours, from 4pm until 10pm that evening, to piece the remains of Mary Kelly back together and inspect the injuries. Her boyfriend, Joe Barnett, was brought in to identify her body and did so by her ears and eyes according to many sources, or by her hair from some others. There was certainly no other facial feature remaining.

Mrs Paumier, who sold roasted chestnuts at the corner of Widegate Street and Sandy's Row (directly to the west of Miller's Court, halfway between Dorset Street and Liverpool Street Station), claimed that a well-dressed man had approached her at about midday on 9 November. He said, 'I suppose you have heard about the

St Leonard's Church, Shoreditch, 1895.

The site of Shoreditch Mortuary, 2006.

Widegate Street, 20 April 1912.

The inquest of Mary Jane Kelly at Shoreditch Town Hall, from *The Pictorial News*, 17 November 1888.

Shoreditch Town Hall, 2006.

murder in Dorset Street?' and, on replying that she had, the man had grinned and continued, 'I know more about it than you'. After staring her in the face, he had then walked down Sandy's Row. While walking away he looked back over his shoulder at Mrs Paumier. She recalled the man was 5ft 6in tall, with a black moustache, and was wearing a black silk hat, a black coat, and speckled trousers. He also carried a black shiny bag, about a foot in depth, and a foot and a half in length. Mrs Paumier stated further that the same man had accosted three young women the previous night. They had asked him what he had in the bag, and he replied, 'Something the ladies don't like!'

The inquest into Mary Jane Kelly's murder was held at Shoreditch Town Hall at the eastern end of Old Street, very close to the church and mortuary, on 12 November 1888.

Henry Wilton (1821–1907) was the sexton of St Leonard's Church and lived at the Clerk's House, next door and to the south (still extant). He bore the cost of Mary Kelly's funeral himself and set up a fund in the hope that people would contribute to it and reimburse his expenses. This was, of course, doomed to failure in an area of such extensive poverty.

May's body was interred in grave 66, row 66, plot 10 of St Patrick's RC Cemetery in Langthorne Road, Leytonstone, on 19 November. No family members were present, although large crowds thronged the streets for the first part of the hearse's journey. Her grave was lost for some years, but a man named John Morrison erected a memorial (at the wrong plot) in 1986. In the early 1990s, the superintendent erected a new memorial at the correct location. To this day, small bottles of gin, plastic flowers, rosaries and ornaments are placed on the spot. In the same graveyard can be found the impressive memorial to John McCarthy and his family and, lost in a sea of other tombs, near the north-western corner lie the remains of Timothy John Evans, the man wrongly executed for two of the murders actually committed by John Christie at 10 Rillington Place, Notting Hill, in the 1940s and 50s.

Dorset Street was renamed Duval Street in 1904 but the murder of Mary Kelly would not be the last there. In 1901 a woman named Mary Ann Austin was stabbed to death at 35 Dorset Street, where Annie Chapman had once lodged. In 1909, another woman named Kitty Ronan was murdered in Elizabeth Prater's old room above 13 Miller's Court. She too had her throat cut. In 1960, a club manager and ex-boxer was shot in the building almost opposite to Miller's Court, next to where George Hutchinson had stood on the night of the Kelly murder.

The burial site of Mary Jane Kelly, 2007.

In 1920, the Corporation of London bought Spitalfields Market to the north and began a long period of expansion and regeneration of the site. The north side of Duval Street, including Miller's Court, came down in 1928. According to the author Leonard Matters, his famous images of the archway were taken just before demolition began in June of that year. The new Fruit Exchange was opened on 30 October 1929. However, the south side of Duval Street remained until the middle of the 1960s. White's Row car park stands in its place and the street today is a private service road. It was not until 1997 that research was undertaken to establish the proximity of the current road to Dorset Street and it was discovered that not only was the current road positioned further north, but it was also on a slightly different axis. Far from the murder spot being underneath thousands of tons of concrete, it was found – and confirmed by recent satellite mapping – that the spot where Mary Jane Kelly died is on the cusp of the current building, across a pillar and a broken kerbstone to its right.

Rose Mylett

Rose Mylett was born in 1862 and, according to her mother, had been married to an upholsterer by the name of Davis. The couple had one son, born in 1881. In the year she died, she had recently split from her husband. The cause is unknown but it was probably due to Rose's drinking.

Rose had lived in various lodging houses over the years. Some had been in the Limehouse and Poplar areas further to the east, but she had also stayed at 18 George Street (where Emma Smith had lodged) and at her mother's own lodgings in Pelham Street (now Woodseer Street), Spitalfields. The street is just north of Hanbury Street and starts at Brick Lane, running east.

Rose had acquired nicknames as well as aliases for herself. She was also known by the names 'Drunken Lizzie' Davis, 'Fair Alice' Downey and Mylett was sometimes changed to Millett or Mellett.

On Wednesday 19 December 1888, Rose Mylett was seen at 7.55pm by Charles Ptolomay, who was a night attendant at Poplar Union Infirmary. She was speaking with two sailors in Poplar High Street, near Clarke's Yard. Rose had the appearance of being sober and Ptolomay heard her saying 'No, no, no!' to one of the men. Their behaviour made him suspicious.

By 2.30am the following morning, Rose was drunk. A woman named Alice Graves spotted her outside the George Tavern in Commercial Road, at the junction with Jubilee Street. She was also in the company of two men.

Rose Mylett's body was found at 4.15am on 20 December by Police Superintendent Robert Golding and Police Constable Thomas Costella. She was discovered in Clarke's Yard, between 186 and 188 Poplar High Street. The body was still quite warm, lying under a wall. Her clothes had

The George Tavern, 2007.

Poplar High Street, *c.*1930. Clarke's Yard entrance is to the right of the cooperage building.
(Courtesy Tower Hamlets Local History Library and Archives)

Poplar High Street, 2007. The location of Clarke's Yard is near to the first car on the left.

not been disarranged in any way and there were no mutilations. She was lying on her left side, her head facing away from the street and her left arm underneath her body. Her right leg was fully extended and her left was slightly drawn up. Golding left Costella at the scene and collected the Divisional Surgeon, Matthew Brownfield, of 171 East India Dock Road. Brownfield's assistant, Dr Harris, went to Clarke's Yard and pronounced life extinct.

Harris searched the body and examined the clothing. Rose was wearing a blue spotted handkerchief around her neck, which was loosely tied. She was clothed in a black alpaca dress, brown stuff skirt, red flannel petticoat, double-breasted dark tweed jacket, lilac print apron, blue and red striped stockings and side-spring boots. She had no hat or bonnet and none was found. In the pocket of her dress he found one shilling in silver and three and a halfpence in bronze, together with a small empty bottle. The woman was about 5ft 2in tall, with hazel eyes and light hair, frizzed close to the head.

Golding felt he had seen the woman before and knew her to be of 'loose character'. After leaving the mortuary where the body had been taken, he returned to Clarke's Yard but was unable to find any trace of a struggle.

Dr Brownfield performed the post-mortem examination. He found the woman to be about 30 years old and well nourished. He noticed mud stains on the front of the left leg. Her eyes were normal and the tongue was not protruding. There were slight marks of blood having extruded from the nostrils and the right side of the nose showed a scratch, which might have been caused by minor violence, while there was an old scar on the left cheek. On the neck there was a mark, which appeared to have been made by a cord, extending from the right side of the spine, around the throat to the lobe of the left ear. Brownfield had, by experimentation, found that a piece of four-fold cord would cause such a mark. He also found marks on the neck that appeared to have been made by thumbs, and index and middle fingers. On trying his own hands in the same positions he found they would probably cause bruising in this way. These marks ran perpendicular to the line that could have been made by a cord. The arms and legs were uninjured. On opening the cranium, he found the brain was engorged with very dark blood. Her lungs were normal and there was recently eaten food in the stomach, but no sign of poison or alcohol. From this examination he concluded that the cause of death was suffocation by strangulation. This could not have been self-inflicted but would most likely have been caused by someone standing behind her and slightly to the left. Brownfield felt the assailant would have wrapped the cord around his hands and thrown the cord over Rose's head, pulling the cord tight and crossing his hands in the

The Illustrated Police News, 5 January 1889.

process. This, he thought, would account for the mark around the neck not forming a complete circle. The cord would have been held in place until death had occurred. Brownfield was sure this was a case of murder.

Assistant Commissioner Robert Anderson did not agree with Brownfield's conclusion and sent Dr Thomas Bond to reexamine the body of Rose Mylett. His assistant, Dr Hibbert, and General Police Surgeon Alexander McKellar inspected the body in advance of this, and all three men agreed with Brownfield's opinion.

Rose was first identified on 23 December, and officially by her mother on Boxing Day, 1888.

On 24 December, Drs Bond and Hibbert met Anderson for a conference during which Anderson expressed the opinion that Rose had not been murdered. That afternoon, Dr Bond returned to Poplar to examine the body personally for a second time. He then met with Anderson and told him that he had changed his mind, now feeling that death had been accidental. He thought Mylett had fallen down whilst drunk and had choked to death on her stiff velvet collar.

Poplar Town Hall, Newby Place, *c*.1870.

The inquest was held at Poplar Town Hall, presided over by Wynne Baxter. It concluded on 9 January 1889 and the official verdict was murder by a person or persons unknown.

ALICE MCKENZIE

Alice McKenzie, like Mary Kelly, had a background that remains unknown. It is believed she was born in around 1849 and was brought up in Peterborough, Cambridgeshire. In 1883 she met a man named John McCormack in Bishopsgate and they lived together in various lodging houses for the six years leading up to Alice's death. Alice was 5ft 4in with a fair complexion and brown hair and eyes. She also had a distinguishing feature: the top of her left thumb was missing as it had been cut off in an industrial accident. Some friends knew her as 'Clay Pipe' Alice, due to her habitual pipe smoking. By 1888, McCormack was working for a Jewish labour employer in Hanbury Street. The couple's last known address was at 52 Gun Street, on the western side, just a little south of Brushfield Street

Mortuary photograph of Alice McKenzie. *(Courtesy Stewart P. Evans)*

and the area of Spitalfields Market. 52 Gun Street was known as Mr Tenpenny's. Though the building has gone, those similar houses directly to its north stood until very recently. A few buildings on the other side of the road still remain, however, and are frequently photographed by the tourists who visit Spitalfields and are surprised to see so many buildings looking as they did a century ago on the south side of Brushfield Street.

Sometime between 3pm and 4pm on Tuesday 16 July 1889, McCormack returned home from his morning shift at work somewhat drunk, and went to bed at Gun Street. He gave Alice one shilling and eightpence to pay Elizabeth Ryder, the lodging-house deputy, for the rent. He also gave her a further shilling to buy some necessities. They had an altercation, which upset Alice. She left the room with the money she had been given, but did not pay the rent.

At 7.10pm Alice took a blind boy by the name of George Dixon for a drink at a pub very close to the Cambridge Theatre. The likelihood is that the pub in question was the Commercial Tavern. It is still in business, near the top of Commercial Street, opposite Commercial Street Police Station. George was later to testify that he had heard Alice in conversation with a man and had asked him

Gun Street from Artillery Lane, 1912. 52 is just past the group of children on the left.
(Courtesy Tower Hamlets Local History Library and Archives)

to buy her a drink. He had agreed, and she soon took George back to the lodging house.

Elizabeth Ryder saw Alice at 8.30pm, leaving 52 Gun Street. She had just been in the kitchen of the lodging house, and was quite drunk. When McCormack woke at 11pm and passed Ryder by the stairs, she informed him that Alice had not paid the rent.

At 11.40pm, a friend who had known Alice for 15 years, named Margaret Franklin, was sitting on some steps by a lodging house. This might either have been her address, which was the notorious White House at 56 Flower and Dean Street, or one in Brick Lane. Franklin was in the company of two other women, who were called Catherine Hughes and Sarah Mahoney. Alice passed the trio, walking at speed towards Whitechapel. Franklin asked her how she was, and she had hurriedly replied, 'All right. I can't stop now'. She was not wearing a bonnet, but did have a light coloured shawl and seemed sober, according to the three women.

Castle Alley in Whitechapel still exists, but has now taken on the name of the rest of the street further to the north. Named Moses and Aaron Road in the early 19th century, it was a fairly minor road, with a yard-wide entrance from the north side of Whitechapel High Street. Castle Alley extended a few hundred feet and then suddenly stopped, turned immediately right and then immediately left again, when it became the far narrower Old Castle Street, finishing at a junction with Wentworth Street. At the kink in the road there was a school on the left-hand side, and further in the direction of Whitechapel High Street there stood the Whitechapel Baths, opened in 1846. Although the main building has been demolished, the façade of the structure marked with a portico

The Commercial Tavern, Commercial Street, 2007.

52 Gun Street, from *The Illustrated Police News*, 27 July 1889.

52 Gun Street, 2007.

The Whitechapel Wash Houses, Castle Alley, 13 January 1938.

reading 'WASH HOUSES', remains and fronts a women's library. The East London Observer describes the street as follows:

> The scene of the murder is probably one of the lowest quarters in the whole of East London , and a spot more suitable for the terrible crime could hardly be found, on account of the evil reputation borne by this particular place, and the absence of any inhabitants in the immediate vicinity. Castle-alley, which is within a quater of a mile of the scenes of the other murders, is principally composed of workshops, and is about 180 yards in length. The thoroughfare itself is blocked up, both day and night, with tradesmen's carts and wagons and costermongers' barrows, while on the opposite side to the workshops or store-houses is a high dead wall, above which, however, are the windows of some dwelling houses. This alley, which is entered by a passage, not more than a yard in width, between Nos 124 and 125, Whitechapel-road, is entirely shut off from view of the main road, and would hardly be observed by the ordinary passer-by. At the end of the passage are the Board School and Whitechapel wash-houses, and the thoroughfare, from the end, leads into Newcastle and Wentworth-streets, both of which are principally occupied by foreign Jews and the frequenters of common lodging-houses. Although the houses in these two streets are densely populated, the people generally enter them from the spitalfields end, especially at night time, on account of the dark and

lonely nature of Castle Alley, as well as the evil reputation it has borne among the respectable portion of the inhabitants. The vans and other vehices which crowd the thoroughfare, notwithstanding the fact that the alley is lighted with three lamps, afford ample cover and secrecy for crime and violence. The exect spot where the body of the murdered woman was found was between two wagons, which were fastened together with chain, outside the premises of Messrs. King and Sons, builders. Right against the wagons was a street lamp, and it was against this the body of the murdered woman was discovered by the police officer. The murderer, on account of the narrowness and intricacy of the surrounding thoroughfares, would have no difficulty in getting away unobserved; and if, as is believed, he is residing in one of the dozen common lodging houses or small houses within a stone's throw of the spot where the deed was committed, he would have no trouble in concealing his identity after making his escape. The woman's character, the nature of the wound, and the scene of the crime, naturally connect this muder with the seven similar murders of last year.

Sometime between 12.15am and 12.30am on 17 July, Sarah Smith (the deputy of the Whitechapel Baths and Wash Houses) retired to her room, overlooking Castle Alley. She began to read, later testifying she heard nothing outside until the blast of a police whistle a little later.

At about 12.25am, PC Joseph Allen 432H was taking a break under a street lamp in Castle Alley, on about the spot where Alice would die less than half an hour later. The alley was, at that time, completely deserted. After five minutes, he left via Wentworth Street. As he walked up Old Castle Street, PC Walter Andrews 272H was entering Castle Alley from Whitechapel High Street. He stayed for about three minutes and also saw nothing out of the ordinary.

At 12.45am it began to rain. Three minutes later, Sergeant Edward Badham met PC Andrews in Old Castle Street. The exchange was limited to little more than 'All right?'.

Just two minutes later, at 12.50am, PC Andrews discovered the body of Alice

The murder site in Castle Alley, from *The Illustrated Police News*, 27 July 1889.

McKenzie by the Whitechapel Baths. She was lying on the pavement close to some market traders' carts, her head angled towards the kerb and her feet towards the wall. Blood was flowing from two stabs in the left side of her neck, and her skirts had been lifted, revealing superficial mutilations to her abdomen, which had cut through the body fat but not pierced the major organs. PC Andrews blew his whistle twice for assistance.

A man named Lewis Jacobs was walking through Castle Alley at that moment, on his way to eat at John McCarthy's place, this being McCarthy of Dorset Street. PC Andrews ordered Jacobs to stay with the body while he went for assistance. He quickly ran into Sergeant Badham again. The whistle had also summoned PC George Neve 101H and PC Joseph Allen 423H. Neve was sent to search the area and Allen to fetch the Inspector on duty and Dr Phillips.

Alice McKenzie's body was removed to the Whitechapel

Old Castle Street looking towards Castle Alley, c.1900.

Castle Alley, 2007. The murder site is on the left, just before the wash houses begin.

Mortuary, where both Drs Thomas Bond and George Bagster Phillips were to examine the corpse. As her body was lifted from the murder scene, it was noted that the ground under her body was dry and, coupled with the fact that blood had still been flowing from the wounds, this indicating she had died some time between 12.25am and 12.45am. Also under her body, the police found a bronze farthing and a clay pipe. This pipe was smashed by accident at the mortuary shortly afterwards.

Detailed inspection of the body revealed that the cause of death had been from severance of the left carotid artery. Two stabs in the left side of the neck dragged slightly forward in the same wound, the cuts having been made from left to right, apparently while the deceased was on the ground. There was some bruising to the chest and five further marks on the left side of the abdomen. A seven-inch long wound ran down her right side to her navel, with several scratches beneath, pointing towards her genitalia, which had been nicked at the top. It was noted that she was also wearing odd stockings.

John McCormack formally identified Alice's body at 2pm the same day, and the inquest was again held at the Working Lads' Institute. She was buried on the 22 or 23 July at Plaistow Cemetery.

The day after the murder, at 8.50pm on 18 July, a man named William Brodie walked into Leman Street Police Station, which was originally built in 1847 and stood halfway down the street towards the Thames, on the western side. A temporary station was in use for a year from 1890 when the original building was demolished, and in 1891 the station was replaced by a larger building on the original site, also occupying the location of the Garrick Theatre next door on the north side. Brodie was very drunk and made a confession to being the murderer of Alice McKenzie. In a statement made to Inspector Henry Moore he claimed to have committed nine murders in Whitechapel.

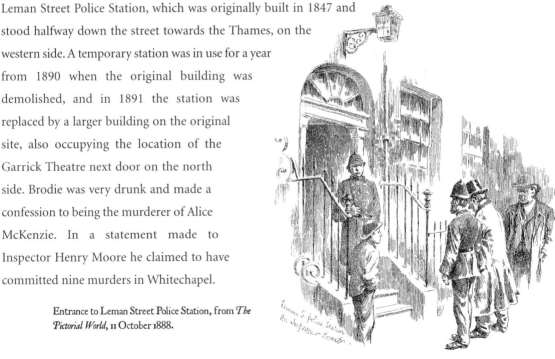

Entrance to Leman Street Police Station, from *The Pictorial World*, 11 October 1888.

It was quickly established that Brodie was of unsound mind. He had been released from prison on 22 August 1888 after serving 11 years of a 14-year sentence for larceny; a case dealt with by the City Police. On his release, he lived at 2 Harvey's Buildings on the Strand. A fortnight later he reported to the Convict Supervision Office that he intended to leave the country and move to the Cape of Good Hope. The day before the McKenzie murder he returned to the Convict Supervision Office with the information that he was back in England and would be residing again at Harvey's Buildings. The Assistant Commissioner wanted to charge him with being a lunatic at large, but when he was brought before the magistrate two days later he was advised to change the charge to the murder of Alice McKenzie. Brodie had been in bed at Harvey's Buildings at the time of the murder although he was remanded until 27 July. Upon release he was quickly rearrested at King's Cross for fraud.

THE PINCHIN STREET TORSO

Many parts of the East End, south of Commercial Road and north of the Thames, still retain plenty of the buildings from the time of the Ripper. Pinchin Street then, as now, ran parallel to Commercial Road, starting just below and to the east of the railway goods depot terminus that once opened out onto that major artery. Christian Street lay to the east and Back Church Lane to the west. Berner Street, the site of the Liz Stride murder, was two minutes walk to the north. Five minutes walk south would bring you to the London Docks. Houses did not begin on Pinchin Street until halfway along its length from the west. The southern side of Pinchin Street consisted almost entirely of dark brick railway arches, as the railway line terminating at nearby Fenchurch Street was directly above. This is still true today, although the arches are now shuttered lock-ups, except for the first one from Back Church Lane, which is entirely bricked up. However, there is private access from business premises on the other side of the arch.

At 5.25am on Tuesday 10 September 1889, PC William Pennett 239H entered Pinchin Street from Christian Street. He was walking along the north side and crossed to the south as the row of arches reached their end. In the final archway, he saw a suspicious-looking bundle. It lay four or five yards in from the pavement, and was close to the right-hand side as Pennett viewed it. The archway was owned by the Whitechapel Board of Works and was filled with paving slabs. It also had an entrance from a yard in Back Church Lane.

PC Pennett approached the bundle and, upon inspecting it, found it to contain a woman's

Pinchin Street, 2007. The torso was found in the first archway on the right.

The discovery of the Pinchin Street torso, from *The Penny Illustrated Paper*, 14 September 1889.

Back Church Lane at the junction with Fairclough Street, 7 April 1909.

The archway, 2007.

torso, covered over with several pieces of rag. The torso was lying on its front, the shoulders towards the near wall. It was very dusty inside the archway but Pennett could not see any footprints or marks left by wheels inside, nor could he see any spots of blood. He chose not to blow his whistle, as he felt it might attract a crowd. Instead, he waited by the body until he saw a passer-by, carrying a broom on his shoulder. Pennett calmly said to him, 'You might go and fetch my mate at the corner'. The man with the broom asked what the problem was and Pennett replied, 'Tell him I have got a job on. Make haste'.

Shortly after the man was sent on his errand, heading up Back Church Lane, two Constables, one of them an Acting Sergeant, ran into Pinchin Street. Pennett asked the Acting Sergeant to fetch the Inspector, as he had discovered a dead body. The Acting Sergeant headed up to Leman Street Police Station, while the other Constable remained at the scene with Pennett.

Pennett left the arch and investigated the other arches in Pinchin Street. Two arches further into the street he saw two sailors. One was asleep and the other had a pipe in his mouth. In the middle archway he found a sleeping shoeblack. All three were taken to Leman Street for questioning.

Inspector Charles Pinhorn soon arrived and ordered an intensive search of the area. On questioning the three men found under the arches, they were found to be completely innocent and released.

Percy John Clark, the assistant to Dr Phillips, arrived at approximately 6am and the body was taken the quarter of a mile south-east to St George's in the East Mortuary. It was felt that death had probably taken place approximately 36 hours earlier on 8 September, the first anniversary of the murder of Annie Chapman in Hanbury Street. Part of Clark's report read:

> It was lying on its anterior surface, with the right arm doubled under the abdomen. The left arm was lying under the left side. The arms were not severed from the body. There was no pool of blood, and there were no signs of any struggle having taken place there. On moving the body I found that there was a little blood underneath where the neck had lain. It was small in quantity and not clotted. The blood had oozed from the cut surface of the neck. Over the surface of the neck and the right shoulder were the remnants of what had been a chemise. It was of common length and such a size as would be worn by a woman of similar build to the trunk found. It had been torn down the front, and had been cut from the front of the armholes on each side. The cuts had apparently been made with a knife. The chemise was bloodstained nearly all over, from being wrapped over the back surface of the neck. There was no clotted blood on it. I could find no distinguishing mark on the chemise. Rigor mortis was not present. Decomposition was just commencing... I found the body appeared to be that of a woman of stoutish build, dark complexion, about 5ft. 3in. in height, and between 30 and 40 years of age... Besides the wounds caused by the severance of the head and legs, there was a wound 15ins. long through the external coat of the abdomen. The body was not bloodstained, except where the chemise had rested upon it. The body had not the appearance of having been recently washed. On the back there were four bruises, all caused before death. There was one over the spine, on a level with the lower part of the shoulder blade. It was about the size of a shilling. An inch lower down there was a similar bruise, about the middle of the back, also on the spine, and that was a bruise about the size of a half-a-crown. On the level of the top of the hip bone was a bruise 2 1/2ins. in diameter. It was such a bruise as would be caused by a fall or a kick. None of the bruises were of old standing. Round the waist was a pale mark and indentation, such as would be caused by clothing during life. On the right arm there were eight distinct bruises and seven on the left, all of them caused before death and of recent date. The back of both forearms and hands were much bruised. On the outer side of the left forearm, about 3in. above the wrist, was a cut about 2in. in length, and half an inch lower down was another cut. These were caused after death. The bruises on the right arm were such as would be

caused by the arms having been tightly grasped. The hands and nails were pallid. The hands did not exhibit any particular kind of work.

Upon searching the area, a bloodstained apron, such as would have been worn by a stout woman, was discovered on a piece of waste ground at Hooper Street, one minute's walk away to the north-west. However, upon examination this was felt to be menstrual blood and the apron had been folded and used as a diaper.

A name was never given to the Pinchin Street Torso, but a popular suggestion at the time was that the remains may have been those of Lydia Hart, a prostitute who had gone missing a week before the discovery. The remains were preserved in the hope that identification might one day be possible and – still preserved – they now lie, unmarked, in a small plot in the East London Cemetery, just yards from the grave of Elizabeth Stride.

Three days before the discovery of the body, on 7 September, a man named John Cleary informed the night editor of the *New York Herald's* London officer that a murder had been committed in Back Church Lane. To compound the mystery, a statement was later taken from a newsvendor in Charing Cross named John Arnold, giving the same address as William Brodie, who had drunkenly confessed to the McKenzie murder. Arnold admitted that he was the man

The burial site of the Pinchin Street torso, 2007.

who had contacted the *New York Herald* and had done so after being told by a soldier in Fleet Street, 'Hurry up with your papers. Another horrible murder in Back Church Lane'. He described the soldier as 35 or 36 years old, 5ft 6in, of fair complexion and with a moustache. He also carried a parcel. Nobody was ever arrested or further suspected of being the killer of the unknown woman.

FRANCES COLES

Frances Coles was the final woman ever seriously suspected of being killed by Jack the Ripper. She was born in 1865 to a respectable bootmaker named James William Coles. She had a secure upbringing and her early years looked promising. Frances had worked for some time at Hora Whinfield & Co. at 58 the Minories (just to the south of the western end of Whitechapel High Street), putting stoppers in bottles for the chemist. This occupation earned her up to seven shillings a week. The work was, however, physically wearing on her knuckles, which caused her pain, and she eventually left the job.

Little is then known of Frances until shortly before she died, by which time she was a hard-drinking prostitute. The decline must have been rapid, as after her death a client named James

Mortuary photograph of Frances Coles.
(Courtesy Stewart P. Evans)

Murray told the police that she had been a prostitute for the previous eight years, since she was approximately 18. She had been working around Whitechapel, Shoreditch and Bow and he had met her at Wilmot's lodging house at 18 Thrawl Street.

Frances tried to keep this lifestyle a secret from her family. When her sister, Mary Ann Coles, invited her for tea on Boxing Day 1890, Frances had told her she was still employed in the Minories chemist and was living with an elderly woman at 42, Richard Street off Commercial Road, though no such address existed. Mary Ann was not convinced by this story, as she observed Frances that looked very poor and dirty, and she could detect alcohol on her breath. Mary Ann was living a respectable single life at 32 Ware Street in Kingsland Road.

By 1891, Frances's father was elderly and was an inmate at Bermondsey Workhouse in Tanner Street. In spite of her personal conditions, Frances visited her father frequently, and often attended church services with him on Sundays. She last saw him on 6 February 1891, exactly a week before she died. Although she now admitted she had left her job, she continued to claim she lived at the non-existent Richard Street address. It was not until Frances was murdered that her father discovered how she had spent the last years of her life.

Thomas Sadler was a 53-year-old merchant seaman and fireman on board the SS *Fez*. He had been discharged on 11 February and made his way from the London Docks up Commercial Street to the Princess Alice pub, today occupying 40–42 on the eastern side, and at the southern junction with Wentworth Street. Though renamed the City Darts, in recent years the pub has reverted to its original title. It was originally built in 1850 and remodelled in 1883 and, until the middle of the 20th century, possessed not only an extra floor, but also a smaller gabled fourth floor with a balustrade and some extremely striking chimneys. It was, at one time, a highly imposing and beautiful building. It was also the hostelry of choice of previous Ripper suspect John Pizer, and has been used for meetings of the Whitechapel Society 1888, the only club in the world dedicated to the study of the Ripper crimes, the East End and Victorian social history in London.

While drinking in the Princess Alice, Sadler had met Frances. They had first encountered each other 18 months previously and Sadler had been a prior client of hers. The two spent the night together in Spitalfields Chambers at 8 White's Row (where Annie/Fanny Millwood had lodged) and spent much of the next day in pubs throughout the area.

Sometime between 7pm and 8pm on Thursday 12 February 1891, Frances had visited a milliner's shop run by Sarah Hawkes at 25 Nottingham Street in Bethnal Green. Nottingham Street ran directly north of Baker's Row and has now been absorbed into Vallance Road, close to Buck's Row/Durward Street, where Mary Ann Nichols died. Frances purchased a black crepe hat for one shilling and elevenpence halfpenny, which Sadler had given her that afternoon. The man who sold Frances the hat, Peter Hawkes, told the police that she had been 'three sheets to the wind', which confirms the stories that she had been drinking all day. Frances kept her old hat and pinned it to her dress.

Between 9pm and 10pm, Frances and Sadler had an argument and went their separate ways. Sadler claimed that the cause of the row was his dissatisfaction with Frances's attitude. He claimed that in Thrawl Street a woman wearing a red shawl had hit him around the head and, as he lay on the ground, a group of men started to kick him. After they ran off into a lodging house, Sadler found his watch and money were missing. He was annoyed that Frances had done nothing to help him.

The Princess Alice, Commercial Street, *c.*1930s. *(Courtesy Truman's Archive)*

The Princess Alice, 2007.

At 10pm, Frances returned to Spitalfields Chambers and sat on a bench in the kitchen, her head resting on her folded arms, drinking herself into a stupor. Sadler followed at 11.30pm, his face cut and bruised. He was understandably in a foul mood and mistook another lodger, Samuel Harris, for the deputy. He said, 'I have been robbed, and if I knew who had done it I would do for them'. He proceeded to show the other lodger his wage certificate for four pounds, 15 shillings and a penny, in the hope this would be a surety for a bed. At midnight, Sadler left the lodging house. Frances remained seated on the bench, slumped over the table, and asleep.

Thomas Sadler got into another fight at 1.15am on Friday 13 February. Trying to force his way back onto the SS *Fez*, he had been set upon by several dockers at the entrance to the London Docks and, upon calling them 'dock rats', he had gained a large scalp wound on the right hand side for his trouble, which was bleeding. He then attempted to enter the Victoria Chambers Lodging House at 40 Upper East Smithfield, but was refused.

At 1.30am, Frances had awoke and left Spitalfields Chambers, as she too had no money. She went straight down towards Wentworth Street where, at Shuttleworth's Eating-House (at 4 Ann

The entrance to the London Docks, 1906.

Street, Wentworth Street, on the south side), she asked Joseph Haswell for a penny-halfpenny's worth of mutton and bread. She was served and sat inside, eating. After a quarter of an hour, Haswell asked her to leave as he wanted to shut up shop. She told him to mind his own business and he was forced to physically eject her. He saw her turning right, in the direction of Brick Lane.

On reaching Commercial Street, Frances met another prostitute called Ellen Callaghan and they walked south, about to turn right at the end to go along Whitechapel High Street in the direction of the Minories. Ellen asked her what she was going to do, but Frances didn't reply. A very short man with a dark moustache, shiny boots and blue trousers, looking like a sailor (but not Sadler) then approached the couple and asked Ellen to go off with him. When she refused he punched her and tore her jacket. Frances stood a few yards off, still fairly drunk, and the man then approached her and asked the same question. Before she answered, Ellen interjected, 'Frances, don't go with that man; I don't like his look'. In spite of what she had just seen, and Ellen's warning, Frances replied that she would. Ellen finished the conversation with 'If you are going with that man I will bid you goodnight'. Ellen left Frances with the short man at the bottom of Commercial Street and walked off to stay at Theobald's lodging house on Brick Lane.

At the same time, three men were walking along Royal Mint Street. It was so named as the extensive Royal Mint buildings lay directly to its south. It also lies just a couple of minutes' walk from the Tower of London. It meets a junction with the Minories on the west and joins onto

Swallow Gardens from Royal Mint Street, September 1961. *(Courtesy Margaret Whitby-Green)*

Cable Street on the east. Beyond its north side, above street level, runs the railway line from Fenchurch Street. Like Pinchin Street, a long row of railway arches, more like passageways, gave access at several points to Chamber Street, running directly parallel on the north side. The men walking along Royal Mint Street were all carmen: William 'Jumbo' Friday and two brothers by the name of Knapton were approaching the Minories along the side closest to the arches. They saw nothing unusual, but did notice a couple standing in a doorway on the other side of the road. They were later identified as being Thomas Fowles and his girlfriend, Kate McCarthy. Friday and the Knaptons said goodnight and parted company.

Swallow Gardens from Chamber Street, from *The Penny Illustrated Paper*, 21 February 1891.

At 2am a policeman, one Sergeant Edwards, saw Sadler – who was drunk and bloody – standing

Swallow Gardens from Chamber Street, September 1961. *(Courtesy Margaret Whitby-Green)*

on the pavement outside the nearby Royal Mint. Edwards passed through Swallow Gardens on the way to the depot and saw nothing unusual.

Swallow Gardens was, by 1891, nothing more than a name. In the early 19th century, before the arrival of the railways, it had been an interesting area containing trees and small gardens around a series of fair-sized houses. These were obliterated as the railway line from Fenchurch Street was constructed in 1854. All that remained was the original title and, by 1891, Swallow Gardens was actually an unoccupied thoroughfare through the railway arch linking Chamber Street to Royal Mint Street. Until recently, most historians had no idea of the correct location of the arch, and wrongly identified Abel's Buildings, an atmospheric narrow alleyway further to the east, close to the bottom of Leman Street, as being the relevant site. Recent research by the authors established the actual location and, with the discovery of the Whitby Collection in April 2007, it was realised that at least one man had known the spot many years before, in 1961. Given the lack of contemporary resources, this shows that Whitby must have been a man who researched his subject deeply and he had consulted period maps rather than relying on the few books that were available on the Whitechapel Murders at that time. Swallow Gardens is a shuttered, private lock-up today and it is not possible to view the actual spot of the murder. That side of Chamber Street,

Swallow Gardens from Chamber Street, 2007.

however, remains to this day a very dark, damp and highly foreboding stretch, even on a bright summer's day. It is probably the most unsettling Ripper-related location of all.

The inquest following the murder was also addressed by a worker who said he had passed through Swallow Gardens at 2.15am and had seen nothing unusual. At the same time, PC Ernest Thompson 240H was on his beat along Chamber Street, having approached from Leman Street. He had

The discovery of Frances Coles's body, from *Le Monde Illustré*, 28 February 1891.

been on the police force for less than two months, and this was his first night walking the beat alone. He heard footsteps walking away towards Mansell Street (at the western end of Chamber Street and running parallel to the Minories, one street further west) but he was not aware if they

The interior of Swallow Gardens, 2007. *(Courtesy Colin Roberts)*

Chamber Street looking towards Leman Street, September **1961.** *(Courtesy Margaret Whitby-Green)*

Chamber Street from Leman Street, September **1961.** *(Courtesy Margaret Whitby-Green)*

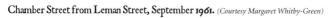

had originated from Swallow Gardens. Seconds later, he turned left into the archway and halfway along he found the body of Frances Coles. She was still alive. Blood was pouring from a severe neck wound and as he shone his lantern on her face, he saw her open and shut one eye. The black crepe hat she had purchased the night before was lying beside her, and her old hat was pinned beneath her dress. Thompson blew on his whistle three times and within a couple of minutes he had been joined by two other policemen, PC Frederick Hart 161H and PC George Elliot 275H. Elliot was in plain clothes. PC Hart went to fetch Dr Frederick John Oxley MRCS from 1 Dock Street, just on the other side of the railway line at the bottom of Leman Street. Oxley arrived at 2.30am and pronounced life extinct.

While Oxley examined the body of Frances Coles, an Inspector Flanagan arrived. When the body was collected and taken away to the Whitechapel Mortuary, he searched the archway and, behind a waterspout, found a folded piece of newspaper, which contained two shillings.

From the examinations conducted by Dr Oxley at the scene and by Dr Phillips at the mortuary, the following conclusions were reached: Frances had been violently thrown to the ground, which had caused wounds to the back of her head. Her throat had been cut while she was on the ground, the killer having held her chin up with his left hand, and cut her throat with his right. There were three cuts, left to right, right to left and left to right again. Oxley believed her throat had only been cut twice as there was one visible wound to the skin but two lacerations to the larynx. Her killer had either struck from the right side or the front, and he had tilted Frances at the moment of cutting her throat so he would not get arterial blood on his clothing. Her clothing was in order and she had not been further mutilated. Dr Phillips was of the opinion that the killer had no anatomical skill. A small part of the victims left ear lobe had been torn off, but this was the result of an earlier injury, perhaps when an earring was ripped out, and was fully healed.

At 3am, Sadler returned to Spitalfields Chambers. He now had a cut to the right cheek and under the left eye. On being refused permission by the deputy, Sarah Fleming, to go into the kitchen because strangers were not allowed, he replied, 'You are a hard-hearted woman'. A little over an hour later, Sadler was seen sitting in a coffeehouse at 19 Whitechapel Road by a man named Joseph Richards.

By 5am, Sadler had arrived in the receiving room of the London Hospital, and a porter named William Fewell noticed him. Sadler had a cut to the scalp and a laceration over one eye. He trimmed the hair from Sadler's scalp wound and washed his face. When asked how he had received the injuries, Sadler answered, 'The truth of it is I have been with a woman and she has done me'.

Mansell Street looking south, 20 April 1914.

Between 6.30 and 7.30am, Sadler was sitting in another coffeehouse at 73 Whitechapel Road with a cup of cocoa. He had asked for coffee, but was refused any on the grounds that he was drunk.

At 10.15am, Duncan Campbell (a seaman at the Sailor's Home in Wells Street) claimed that he had purchased a knife from Sadler for one shilling and some tobacco. The knife was so blunt that Thomas Robinson, a marine stores dealer who eventually purchased the knife from Campbell, had to sharpen it before he could use it at dinner.

The following day, Saturday 14 February, Sadler was arrested in the street. Samuel Harris was in the company of Detective Sergeant Don and Detective Gill, assisting them in the search. Harris spotted Sadler in the Phoenix pub and went outside to inform the policemen. Gill went in and asked Sadler to come out, at which point he was taken to Leman Street Police Station.

Sadler was the obvious and immediate suspect in the Coles murder case and, because of this, there were also strong suspicions that he was Jack the Ripper. The evidence of Sergeant Edwards, and of Sarah Fleming – who had seen how inebriated Sadler was at both 2am and 3am – showed it was unlikely that Sadler would have been able to commit the murder as at times he was barely able to stand. On 3 March 1891, he was acquitted of the murder of Frances Coles.

The inquest was again held at the Working Lads' Institute on Whitechapel Road and the verdict reached was the only one possible: murder by a person or persons unknown.

On 1 December 1900, a man named Barnet Abrahams murdered PC Ernest Thompson, who had discovered the body of Frances Coles on his first night on the beat. Thompson was stabbed after stopping antisocial behaviour by Abrahams and others. Thompson had been in the police force for 10 years and left a wife and four children.

Afterword

The death of Frances Coles marked the end of the Whitechapel Murders. A middle-aged prostitute named Carrie Brown was killed and mutilated in a down-at-heel hotel room in New York two months later, but this is a footnote to the crimes.

Why did the killer stop? Serial killers choosing to end their murder sprees are very rare creatures indeed. They include Bela Kiss, who killed two dozen women in Hungary in the early 20th century, the English serial killers Fred and Rosemary West and most recently Dennis Rader, who went by the name BTK (bind, torture, kill) in America. Generally, if murders stop somewhere, the killer relocates (there is no real evidence to suggest that is the case here), dies (a possibility), or is incarcerated for a lesser felony.

Today, many Ripper historians favour the final option. Many killers have been identified after being arrested for petty crimes; Ted Bundy was caught for speeding and Leonard Lake committed suicide after being taken into custody for shoplifting. It is possible that the Ripper could have been arrested for some small crime, went mad while incarcerated and was sent to an asylum, where he died undetected. If this is the case, the most likely location for the Ripper to have spent

Colney Hatch, 2006.

9 King's Bench Walk, 2007.

his last days is Colney Hatch lunatic asylum in Friern Barnet. This is where a potential – but ultimately unlikely – Ripper suspect by the name of Aaron Kosminski was taken in 1891.

Hundreds of potential suspects have been presented over the years. Most people are aware of the Royal Conspiracy, naming Queen Victoria's grandson, Prince Eddy, or the physician Sir William Gull. Others will have heard of the futile attempts by the author Patricia Cornwell to prove the artist Walter Sickert was the killer. Yet more will have heard some vague mention of Jack the Ripper having written a diary. This is the notorious Maybrick Diary, supposedly written by the Liverpool cotton merchant, James Maybrick. Until recent years he was known as a murder victim rather than a killer himself. Today, few serious researchers believe the Diary to be anything other than a fake. Having reached a general consensus, the debate is now about who faked it and when it was done. Yet another suspect, popular some years ago, was the barrister and schoolteacher Montague John Druitt, who had chambers at 9 King's Bench Walk. It seems he was only ever seriously suspected because he committed suicide shortly after the murder of Mary Jane Kelly, and it has recently been confirmed that during the times of most of the murders, he was out of London playing cricket.

Ripper studies have reached such a level that some students of the case have even gone so far as to study the phases of the moon on the nights in question, not as part of some astrology chart, but simply to see how much light the killer would have had to work by. The analysis of the case has got that intense.

In truth, all we can really say about Jack the Ripper is that he would have been a local man – the East End was a rat-run of alleyways, and this is probably how he always managed to evade capture. He would also almost certainly have had his own room to go back to each night. If he were sharing with other people, they would have noticed the blood all over his clothes when he arrived. On the streets, it was dark. Men wore dark suits, and blood would not have been apparent unless someone was closely inspected.

The Ripper was probably a faceless nobody who, by day, may have led a normal and mundane existence but, at night, occasionally, something would trigger a murderous frenzy, and the next day his friends – and maybe family – would be none the wiser. It is not a million miles away from serial killers in the 21st century.

BIBLIOGRAPHY

Begg, Paul, *Jack the Ripper: The Facts*, Robson (London), 2004.

Begg, Paul, Martin Fido, and Keith Skinner, *The Jack the Ripper A-Z*, Headline (London), revised edition 1996.

Eddleston, John J., *Jack the Ripper: An Encyclopaedia*, Metro (London), 2002.

Evans, Stewart P., and Keith Skinner, *The Ultimate Jack the Ripper Sourcebook*, Robinson (London), 2001.

Evans, Stewart P., and Keith Skinner, *Jack the Ripper: Letters from Hell*, Alan Sutton (Stroud), 2004.

Evans, Stewart P., and Donald Rumbelow, *Jack the Ripper: Scotland Yard Investigates*, Alan Sutton (Stroud), 2006.

Jones, Richard, *Uncovering Jack the Rippers London*, New Holland (London), 2007.

London, Jack, *The People of the Abyss*, Grosset & Dunlap (New York), 1907.

McLaughlin, Robert J., *The First Jack the Ripper Victim Photographs*, Zwerghaus, 2005.

Rumbelow, Donald, *The Complete Jack the Ripper*, Penguin (London), 2004.

Sims, George R. (editor), *Living London*, Cassell & Co. Ltd (London), 1901 to 1903.

Sheldon, Neal, *Jack the Ripper and His Victims*, Privately published (Hornchurch), 1999.

Sheppard, F. H. W., 'general editor', *Survey of London: Spitalfields and Mile End New Town*, Athlone Press (London), 1957.

Sugden, Philip, *The Complete History of Jack the Ripper*, Robinson (London), 2002.

Maps Consulted

Whitechapel, Spitalfields and The Bank, Ordnance Survey, 1873, 1894 and 1913.

Poplar, Ordnance Survey, 1894.

Bethnal Green, Ordnance Survey 1894.

Shoreditch, Ordnance Survey 1893.

Bacon's New Large Scale Ordnance Atlas of London & Suburbs, 1888.

Goad's Fire Insurance Plans, Various years.